The Bhagavad Gita
According to Gandhi

Berkeley Hills Books
Titles by M K Gandhi

The Bhagavad Gita According to Gandhi

Book of Prayers

Prayer

Vows and Observances

The Way to God

The Bhagavad Gita
According to Gandhi

MOHANDAS K. GANDHI

Text and commentary translated from Gujarati
Edited by John Strohmeier

Berkeley Hills Books
Berkeley, California

Published by
Berkeley Hills Books
P. O. Box 9877
Berkeley, California 94709
www.berkeleyhills.com
(888) 848-7303

Comments on this book may also be addressed to:
jpstroh@berkeleyhills.com

Cover design by Elysium, San Francisco.
Cover Photo: Margaret Bourke-White/LIFE/TimePix.
Manufactured in the United States of America.
Distributed by Publishers Group West.
First Printing, August 2000.

Library of Congress Cataloging-in-Publication Data

Gandhi, Mahatma, 1869-1948.
  The Bhagavad Gita according to Gandhi / Mohandas K. Gandhi ; text
and
commentary translated from Gujarati ; edited by John Strohmeier.
     p. cm.
Includes bibliographical references (p.) and index.
  ISBN I-893163-11-3 (Pbk.)
  I. Strohmeier, John. II. Title.
  BLI138.6.G36 2000
  294.5'92404521--dc21

                                            00-010376

Contents

Foreword

MICHAEL NAGLER

To write some words of introduction to this book is an honor I scarcely deserve. Millions believe, myself among them, that Mahatma Gandhi was the greatest human being to have walked through the turbulent pages of the twentieth century. And as for the Gita, its wisdom is unrivalled. As Julien Green says of the Christian Gospels in his biography of St. Francis, "The book has a peculiar feature: You can listen to it year after year, and then a moment comes when from out of its pages comes a soundless, but deafening voice that you will never be able to silence." I have had such moments reading the Gita, as have millions of others.

It is important to grasp the relationship between this man and this book, this love-match between person and scripture. For Gandhi, the Gita's was a voice that changes forever the way one understands things, the source of a profound shift in behavior and vision. He describes, for example, how he was once almost undone by worldly concerns when a verse of the Gita — chapter two, verse 15 — came to him, "and the very next moment I was almost dancing with relief."

Such experiences do not come for the mere reading. Great as is the truth of the Gita, or any scripture, the readiness is all. "The soil of our mind has to be cultivated for the seed of the truth to take such hold." That comment of Gandhi comes shortly before a section — the last eighteen verses of the second chapter — on which he practiced meditation nearly every day of his adult life. In his morning and evening prayer meetings, Gandhi would use these verses to bring his mind to a standstill — a state of utmost receptivity to Truth. We might ascribe such a reaction to faith, and that's not wrong. But faith doesn't come unbidden, it requires systematic cultivation.

In the modern era, there's a tendency to think that this cultivation is intellectual. That would be true if the purpose were merely to understand the scripture. But for Gandhi, understanding was only an adjunct to self-realization, almost an unnecessary one. The point is not just to understand, but to absorb, so that one unconsciously acts out the truth absorbed. "At the back of my reading [of the Gita] there is the claim of an endeavor to enforce the meaning in my own conduct for an unbroken period of forty years." And he adds, quoting a proverb from Indian tradition, "one may cast into the river a ton of thoughts and cling to an ounce of practice."

The good news is that no one lacks the endowment to find a practice. Intellectually we may not all be Einsteins, just as spiritually we may not all be born, as my teacher, Sri Eknath Easwaran, used to say, "with a spiritual spoon in our mouth." But what the Gita teaches (and Gandhi unwaveringly did) is that by finding the right work and plugging away at it with determination, anyone can improve their capacity to absorb Truth. From this teaching I draw no small comfort.

If one wanted to pick the single hallmark of Gandhi's behavior by which the sign of the Gita's influence could be read, it would almost certainly be desireless action. This requires a word of explanation. What one doesn't desire in this state is not an opportunity to act, nor that his or her action should do good. It's *phalam*, usually translated the "fruit" of one's action. This is literally correct, but more precisely it means that result which benefits us personally.

Gandhi gives two superb illustrations of this elusive discrimination and why it is crucial that we make it. Is it wrong to be attached to a positive goal — say, to the one he was fighting for with every ounce of his life's strength? "Yes," he answers, "[for] if we are attached to our goal of winning liberty, we shall not hesitate to adopt bad means." Gandhi also collected millions of rupees from millions of individuals for the purpose of winning this goal, but, he maintained, "if a person is particular that he would give coins to me personally," either out of attachment to Gandhi himself or out of a desire for recognition, "one day he might even steal them." This subtle principle perhaps explains all of Gandhi, if one knew how to apply it.

I might give just one further illustration before stepping aside for the reader to draw his or her own conclusions, and benefits, from this remarkable book. One can be attached (in the negative sense) even to the highest truth Gandhi espoused — nonviolence. Nonviolence can become a mood rather than a power, a congratulatory way one thinks about oneself. When that happens, the belief in nonviolence is only that — a belief, not an opening of ourselves to the inner forces of Truth. Hence, Gandhi explained, we see the seemingly contradictory posture of the Gita's Krishna, who urges the hero Arjuna, who represents you and me in his spiritual crisis and befuddlement, to fight while holding aloft the banner of nondiscrimination and nonviolence. "Even if we believe in nonviolence, it would not be proper for us to refuse, through cowardice, to protect the weak." How do we know whether we're refusing out of cowardice or nonviolence? That only a lifetime of practice can help us decide.

Editor's Note

JOHN STROHMEIER

Gandhi's Text and Commentary

The Bhagavad Gita According to Gandhi is based upon talks given by Mahatma Gandhi at Satyagraha Ashram in Ahmedabad, India between February 24 and November 27, 1926. During this time — a period of withdrawal from mass political activity — Gandhi devoted much of his energy to translating the Gita from Sanskrit into his native Gujarati. This effort inspired him to address his followers almost daily, after morning prayer sessions, about its content and meaning as it unfolded before him.

Gandhi's commentary was transcribed on the spot by his amanuensis, Mahadev Desai, and at least one other resident of the ashram, Punjabhai, but not until 1955 was it published in its entirety, in Gujarati. It first appeared in English in *The Collected Works of Mahatma Gandhi*, published by the Government of India in 1969. It is widely regarded as among the most important commentaries on the Gita produced in India in the twentieth century, alongside those of B. G. Tilak, Sri Aurobindo and Sarvepalli Radhakrishnan

For this edition, in an effort to bring forward and clarify the essence of Gandhi's thinking, I have abridged the commentary considerably, and rearranged it in a few sections. The original presentation of the material was unrehearsed and relatively spontaneous, and includes many of the redundancies, contradictions, ellipses, false starts and situational digressions of everyday conversation. Some of these I have deleted after pursuing the trail of Gandhi's thought carefully and respectfully. (Among these deletions is one from chapter eight, lines 9-10, where Gandhi observes that one who "keeps his mouth shut" attains to the realm of the Supreme; certainly a comment to the restless boys in his audience.)

Others I have let stand where they illuminated important ideas, or explained the context in which he made his remarks. For example, his references to an impending flood, the killing of a snake and the tormenting of a dog by some boys, although quite specific to ashram events, carry lessons that apply to the world beyond the ashram walls.

About the Gita

The Bhagavad Gita, "The Song of the Lord," is a 700-line section of a much longer Sanskrit war epic, the Mahabharata. The Mahabharata tells the story of a legendary conflict between two branches of an Indian ruling family that may have taken place between 1000 and 700 B.C. Authorship of the poem is traditionally ascribed to Vyasa, who perhaps lived between the fifth and third centuries B.C.

In the Mahabharata, Pandu, the King of Hastinapura, leaves his throne and retires to the forest in a response to a curse, never to return. In his absence his elder brother, the blind Dhritirashtra, is to act as Regent, presumably until Pandu's son, Yudhishthira, is old enough to assume the role of king. Over time, Dhritirashtra comes to prefer that his own son, Duryodhana, become king in Yudhishthira's place. The battle between Duryodhana and his followers (the Kauravas) and the supporters of Yudhishthira (the Pandavas) for rule of Hastinapura sets the scene for the Bhagavad Gita.

Nearly the entire text of the Bhagavad Gita is a conversation between Krishna, an incarnation of the god Vishnu, and Arjuna, Yudhishthira's brother and General of the Pandava army. Krishna is Arjuna's charioteer. Their conversation takes place in the middle of the battlefield just as fighting is about to begin.

The first few lines of the Gita can be somewhat confusing because the entire conversation between Krishna and Arjuna is presented as reported speech. The blind Regent Dhritirashtra asks his Prime Minister, Sanjaya, to describe for him the progress of the battle. Although they are far from the battlefield, Sanjaya is granted the power of divine sight in order that he might observe and relate to Dhritisrashtra the defeat of his sons.

Editing Notes

The text and commentary presented here are taken almost entirely from the *Collected Works of Mahatma Gandhi*, volume XXXII (1926-1927), pages 94-376, "Discourses on the Gita". The names of those who executed the translation from Gandhi's Gujarati into English for the *Collected Works* are not listed, although the translation of the text of the Gita itself follows, with only slight variation, Mahadev Desai's edition (see bibliography), which was proofed and authorized by Gandhi. Additional commentary on a few verses is taken from the very limited notes Gandhi inserted in Desai's important work.

A number of Sanskrit words, such as *yajna*, *bhakti* and *karma*, are generally not translated because no satisfactory equivalents exist in English. These words are printed in italics and defined in the glossary at the back of the book, along with a list of epithets used for Krishna and Arjuna. Note that parentheses in the text are, without exception, Gandhi's notations, while the occasional clarifications and definitions I have inserted are set off by square brackets.

Acknowledgements

I would like to thank for their ideas and encouragement Robert Dobbin, Daniel Peckham, Laura Pérez and Michael Nagler. I am also indebted to the late Eknath Easwaran for his inspiration to explore the works of Mahatma Gandhi, and to those gifted editors who have produced previous editions of Gandhi's Gita writings: Mahadev Desai and Narahari Parikh.

Introduction

M K GANDHI

This introduction was written in 1929 to accompany Gandhi's Gujarati translation of the Bhagavad Gita. He later translated the essay into English, and published it in 1931 in the pages of his periodical, Young India, *under the title,* Anasaktiyoga: The Gospel of Selfless Action.

I. Just as, acted upon by the affection of coworkers like Swami Anand and others, I wrote my [autobiography] *Experiments with Truth*, so has it been regarding my rendering of the Gita. "We shall be able to appreciate your meaning of the message of the Gita, only when we are able to study a translation of the whole text by yourself, with the addition of such notes as you may deem necessary. I do not think it is just on your part to deduce *ahimsa* [nonviolence] from stray verses." Thus spoke Swami Anand to me during the noncooperation days. I felt the force of his remarks. I, therefore, told him that I would adopt his suggestions when I got the time. Shortly afterwards I was imprisoned. During my incarceration I was able to study the Gita more fully. I went through the Gujarati translation of the Lokamanya's [B. G. Tilak's] great work. He had kindly presented me with the Marathi original and the translations in Gujarati and Hindi, and had asked me, if I could not tackle the original, at least to go through the Gujarati translation. I had not been able to follow the advice outside the prison walls. But when I was imprisoned I read the Gujarati translation. This reading whetted my appetite for more and I glanced through several works on the Gita.

2. My first acquaintance with the Gita began in 1888-89 with the verse translation by Sir Edwin Arnold known as *The Song Celestial*. On reading it I felt a keen desire to read a Gujarati translation. And I read as many translations as I could lay hold of. But all such reading can give me no passport for presenting my own translation. Then again my knowledge of Sanskrit is limited; my knowledge of Gujarati too is in no way scholarly. How could I then dare present the public with my translation?

3. It has been my endeavor, as also that of some companions, to reduce to practice the teaching of the Gita as I understood it. The Gita has become for us a spiritual reference book. I am aware that we ever fail to act in perfect accord with the teaching. The failure is not due to want of effort, but is in spite of it. Even through the failures we seem to see rays of hope. The accompanying rendering contains the meaning of the Gita message this little band is trying to enforce in daily conduct.

4. Again this rendering is designed for women, the commercial class, the so-called Sudras [the lowest of the four castes] and the like, who have little or no literary equipment, who have neither the time nor the desire to read the Gita in the original, and yet who stand in need of its support. In spite of my Gujarati being unscholarly, I must own to having the desire to leave to the Gujaratis, through the mother tongue, whatever knowledge I may possess. I do indeed wish that at a time when literary output of a questionable character is pouring in upon the Gujaratis, they should have before them a rendering the majority can understand of a book that is regarded as unrivaled for its spiritual merit and so withstand the overwhelming flood of unclean literature.

5. This desire does not mean any disrespect to the other renderings. They have their own place. But I am not aware of

the claim made by the translators of enforcing their meaning of the Gita in their own lives. At the back of my reading there is the claim of an endeavor to enforce the meaning in my own conduct for an unbroken period of forty years. For this reason I do indeed harbor the wish that all Gujarati men or women, wishing to shape their conduct according to their faith, should digest and derive strength from the translation here presented.

6. My coworkers, too, have worked at this translation. My knowledge of Sanskrit being very limited, I should not have full confidence in my literal translation. To that extent, therefore, the translation has passed before the eyes of Vinoba, Kaka Kalelkar, Mahadev Desai and Kishorlal Mashruvala.

7. Now about the message of the Gita.

8. Even in 1888-89, when I first became acquainted with the Gita, I felt that it was not a historical work, but that, under the guise of physical warfare, it described the duel that perpetually went on in the hearts of mankind, and that physical warfare was brought in merely to make the description of the internal duel more alluring. This preliminary intuition became more confirmed on a closer study of religion and the Gita. A study of the Mahabharata gave it added confirmation. I do not regard the Mahabharata as a historical work in the accepted sense. By ascribing to the chief actors superhuman or subhuman origins, the great Vyasa [author of the Mahabharata] made short work of the history of kings and their peoples. The persons therein described may be historical, but the author of the Mahabharata has used them merely to drive home his religious theme.

9. The author of the Mahabharata has not established the necessity of physical warfare; on the contrary he has proved its futility. He has made the victors shed tears of sorrow and repentance, and has left them nothing but a legacy of miseries.

10. In this great work the Gita is the crown. Its second chapter, instead of teaching the rules of physical warfare, tells us how a perfected man is to be known. In the characteristics of the perfected man of the Gita, I do not see any to correspond to physical warfare. Its whole design is inconsistent with the rules of conduct governing the relations between warring parties.

11. Krishna of the Gita is perfection and right knowledge personified; but the picture is imaginary. That does not mean that Krishna, the adored of his people, never lived. But perfection is imagined. The idea of a perfect incarnation is an aftergrowth.

12. In Hinduism, incarnation is ascribed to one who has performed some extraordinary service of mankind. All embodied life is in reality an incarnation of God, but it is not usual to consider every living being an incarnation. Future generations pay this homage to one who, in his own generation, has been extraordinarily religious in his conduct. I can see nothing wrong in this procedure; it takes nothing from God's greatness, and there is no violence done to Truth. There is an Urdu saying which means, "Adam is not God but he is a spark of the Divine." And therefore he who is the most religiously behaved has most of the divine spark in him. It is in accordance with this train of thought that Krishna enjoys, in Hinduism, the status of the most perfect incarnation.

13. This belief in incarnation is a testimony of man's lofty spiritual ambition. Man is not at peace with himself till he has become like unto God. The endeavor to reach this state is supreme, the only ambition worth having. And this is self-realization. This self-realization is the subject of the Gita, as it is of all scriptures. But its author surely did not write it to establish that doctrine. The object of the Gita appears to me to be that of

showing the most excellent way to attain self-realization. That which is to be found, more or less clearly, spread out here and there in Hindu religious books, has been brought out in the clearest possible language in the Gita even at the risk of repetition.

14. That matchless remedy [i.e. the way to self-realization] is renunciation of fruits of action.

15. This is the center round which the Gita is woven. This renunciation is the central sun round which devotion, knowledge and the rest revolve like planets. The body has been likened to a prison. There must be action where there is body. Not one embodied being is exempted from labor. And yet all religions proclaim that it is possible for man, by treating the body as the temple of God, to attain freedom. Every action is tainted, be it ever so trivial. How can the body be made the temple of God? In other words how can one be free from action, i.e. from the taint of sin? The Gita has answered the question in decisive language: By desireless action; by renouncing fruits of action; by dedicating all activities to God, i.e., surrendering oneself to Him body and soul.

16. But desirelessness or renunciation does not come for the mere talking about it. It is not attained by an intellectual feat. It is attainable only by a constant heart-churn. Right knowledge is necessary for attaining renunciation. Learned men possess a knowledge of a kind. They may recite the Vedas from memory, yet they may be steeped in self-indulgence. In order that knowledge may not run riot, the author of the Gita has insisted on devotion accompanying it and has given it the first place. Knowledge without devotion will be like a misfire. Therefore, says the Gita, "Have devotion, and knowledge will follow." This devotion is not mere lip worship, it is a wrestling with

death. Hence the Gita's assessment of the devotee's qualities is similar to that of the sage's.

17. Thus the devotion required by the Gita is no soft-hearted effusiveness. It certainly is not blind faith. The devotion of the Gita has the least to do with externals. A devotee may use, if he likes, rosaries, forehead marks, make offerings, but these things are no test of his devotion. He is the devotee who is jealous of none, who is a fount of mercy, who is without egotism, who is selfless, who is ever forgiving, who is always contented, whose resolutions are firm, who has dedicated mind and soul to God, who causes no dread, who is not afraid of others, who is free from exultation, sorrow and fear, who is pure, who is versed in action and yet remains unaffected by it, who renounces all fruit, good or bad, who treats friend and foe alike, who is untouched by respect or disrespect, who is not puffed up by praise, who does not go under when people speak ill of him, who loves silence and solitude, who has a disciplined reason. Such devotion is inconsistent with the existence at the same time of strong attachments.

18. We thus see, that to be a real devotee is to realize oneself. Self-realization is not something apart. One rupee can purchase us poison or nectar, but knowledge or devotion cannot buy us either salvation or bondage. These are not media of exchange. They are themselves the thing we want. In other words, if the means and the end are not identical, they are almost so. The extreme means is salvation. Salvation of the Gita is perfect peace.

19. But such knowledge and devotion, to be true, have to stand the test of renunciation of fruits of action. Mere knowledge of right and wrong will not make one fit for salvation. According to common notions, a mere learned man will pass as

a *pandit*. He need not perform any service. He will regard it as bondage even to lift a little iota.

20. Or take *bhakti*. The popular notion of *bhakti* is soft-heartedness, telling beads and the like, and disdaining to do even a loving service, lest the telling of beads, etc. might be interrupted. This *bhakti*, therefore, leaves the rosary only for eating, drinking, and the like, never for grinding corn or nursing patients.

21. But the Gita says, "No one has attained his goal without action. Even men like Janaka attained salvation through action. If even I were lazily to cease working, the world would perish. How much more necessary then for the people at large to engage in action?"

22. While on the one hand it is beyond dispute that all action binds, on the other hand it is equally true that all living beings have to do some work, whether they will or no. Here all activity, whether mental or physical, is to be included in the term action. Then how is one to be free from the bondage of action, even though he may be acting? The manner in which the Gita has solved the problem is, to my knowledge, unique. The Gita says, "Do your allotted work but renounce its fruit. Be detached and work. Have no desire for reward and work."

23. This is the unmistakable teaching of the Gita. He who gives up action falls. He who gives up only the reward rises. But renunciation of the fruit in no way means indifference to the result. In regard to every action one must know the result that is expected to follow, the means thereto, and the capacity for it. He, who, being thus equipped, is without desire for the result, and is yet wholly engrossed in the due fulfillment of the task before him, is said to have renounced the fruits of his action.

24. Again, let no one consider renunciation to mean want

of fruit for the renouncer. The Gita reading does not warrant such a meaning. Renunciation means absence of hankering after fruit. As a matter of fact, he who renounces reaps a thousandfold. The renunciation of the Gita is the acid test of faith. He who is ever brooding over result often loses nerve in the performance of his duty. He becomes impatient and then gives vent to anger and begins to do unworthy things; he jumps from action to action, never remaining faithful to any. He who broods over results is like a man given to objects of senses; he is ever distracted, he says good-bye to all scruples, everything is right in his estimation and he therefore resorts to means fair and foul to attain his end.

25. From the bitter experiences of desire for fruit the author of the Gita discovered the path of renunciation of fruit and put it before the world in a most convincing manner. The common belief is that religion is always opposed to material good. "One cannot act religiously in mercantile and other such matters. There is no place for religion in such pursuits. Religion is only for attainment of salvation," we hear many worldly-wise people say. In my opinion the author of the Gita has dispelled this delusion. He has drawn no line of demarcation between salvation and worldly pursuits. On the contrary he has shown that religion must rule even our worldly pursuits. I have felt that the Gita teaches us that what cannot be followed out in day-to-day practice cannot be called religion. Thus, according to the Gita, all acts that are incapable of being performed without attachment are taboo. This golden rule saves mankind from many a pitfall. According to this interpretation murder, lying, dissoluteness and the like must be regarded as sinful and therefore taboo. Man's life then becomes simple, and from that simpleness springs peace.

26. Thinking along these lines, I have felt that in trying to enforce in one's life the central teaching of the Gita, one is bound to follow Truth and *ahimsa* [nonviolence]. When there is no desire for fruit, there is no temptation for untruth or *himsa*. Take any instance of untruth or violence, and it will be found that at its back was the desire to attain the cherished end. But it may be freely admitted that the Gita was not written to establish *ahimsa*. It was an accepted and primary duty even before the Gita age. The Gita had to deliver the message of renunciation of fruit. This is clearly brought out as early as the second chapter.

27. But if the Gita believed in *ahimsa* or it was included in desirelessness, why did the author take a warlike illustration? When the Gita was written, although people believed in *ahimsa*, wars were not only not taboo, but nobody observed the contradiction between them and *ahimsa*.

28. In assessing the implications of renunciation of fruit, we are not required to probe the mind of the author of the Gita as to his limitations of *ahimsa* and the like. Because a poet puts a particular truth before the world, it does not necessarily follow that he has known or worked out all its great consequences, or that having done so, he is able always to express them fully. In this perhaps lies the greatness of the poem and the poet. A poet's meaning is limitless. Like man, the meaning of great writings suffers evolution. On examining the history of languages, we notice that the meaning of important words has changed or expanded. This is true of the Gita. The author has himself extended the meanings of some current words. We are able to discover this even on a superficial examination. It is possible that, in the age prior to that of the Gita, offering animals in sacrifice was permissible. But there is not a trace of it in the sacrifice in the Gita sense. In the Gita continuous concentration

on God is the king of sacrifices. The third chapter seems to show that sacrifice chiefly means body-labor for service. The third and fourth chapters read together will give us other meanings for sacrifice, but never animal-sacrifice. Similarly has the meaning of the word *sannyasa* [renunciation] undergone, in the Gita, a transformation. The *sannyasa* of the Gita will not tolerate complete cessation of all activity. The *sannyasa* of the Gita is all work and yet no work. Thus the author of the Gita, by extending meanings of words, has taught us to imitate him. Let it be granted that, according to the letter of the Gita, it is possible to say that warfare is consistent with renunciation of fruit. But after forty years' unremitting endeavor fully to enforce the teaching of the Gita in my own life, I have, in all humility, felt that perfect renunciation is impossible without perfect observance of *ahimsa* in every shape and form.

29. The Gita is not an aphoristic work; it is a great religious poem. The deeper you dive into it, the richer the meanings you get. It being meant for the people at large, there is pleasing repetition. With every age the important words will carry new and expanding meanings. But its central teaching will never vary. The seeker is at liberty to extract from this treasure any meaning he likes so as to enable him to enforce in his life the central teaching.

30. Nor is the Gita a collection of Dos and Don'ts. What is lawful for one may be unlawful for another. What may be permissible at one time, or in one place, may not be so at another time, and in another place. Desire for fruit is the only universal prohibition. Desirelessness is obligatory.

31. The Gita has sung the praises of knowledge, but is beyond the mere intellect. It is essentially addressed to the heart and capable of being understood by the heart. Therefore the

Gita is not for those who have no faith. The author makes Krishna say, "Do not entrust this treasure to him who is without sacrifice, without devotion, without the desire for this teaching and who denies Me. On the other hand, those who will give this precious treasure to My devotees will, by the fact of this service, assuredly reach Me. And those who, being free from malice, will with faith absorb this teaching, shall, having attained freedom, live where people of true merit go after death."

The Bhagavad Gita
According to Gandhi

Chapter One

The Mahabharata is not history. It is a work treating of religious and ethical questions. The battle described here is a struggle between *dharma* [duty, right conduct] and *adharma* [its opposite]. It is a battle between the innumerable forces of good and evil, which become personified in us as virtues and vices. The Kauravas represent the forces of Evil, the Pandavas the forces of Good. We shall leave aside the question of violence and nonviolence and say that this work was written to explain man's duty in this inner strife.

Dhritarashtra said:

(1) Tell me, O Sanjaya, what my sons and Pandu's, assembled, on battle intent, did on the field of Kuru, the field of duty.

Sanjaya said:

(2) On seeing the Pandavas' army drawn up in battle array, King Duryodhana approached Drona, the preceptor, and addressed him thus:

(3) Behold, O preceptor, this mighty army of the sons of Pandu, set in array by the son of Drupada, thy wise disciple.

(4) Here are brave bowmen, peers of Bhima and Arjuna in fighting — Yuyudhana and Virata, and the *maharatha* [great charioteer] Drupada,

(5) Drishtaketu, Chekitana, valorous Kashiraja, Purujit the Kuntibhoja, and Shaibya, chief among men,

(6) Valiant Yudhamanyu, valorous Uttamaujas, Subhadhra's son, and the sons of Draupadi — each one of them a *maharatha.*

(7) Acquaint thyself now, O best of *Brahmanas,* with the distinguished among us. I mention, for thy information, the names of the captains of my army:

(8) Thy noble self, Bhishma, Karna, and Kripa, victorious in battle, Ashvatthaman, Vikarna, also Somadatta's son.

Whether out of compassion for Duryodhana [the leader of the Kauravas], or because he was generous-hearted, Karna joined the former's side. Besides Karna, Duryodhana had good men like Bhishma and Drona also on his side. This suggests that evil cannot by itself flourish in this world. It can do so only if it is allied with some good. This was the principle underlying noncooperation — that the evil system which the [British colonial] Government represents, and which has endured only because of the support it receives from good people, cannot survive if that support is withdrawn.

(9) There is many another hero, known for his skill in wielding diverse weapons, pledged to lay down his life for my sake, and all adepts in war.

(10) This our force, commanded by Bhishma, is all too inadequate; while theirs, commanded by Bhima, is quite adequate.

(11) Therefore, let each of you, holding your appointed places, at every entrance, guard only Bhishma.

(12) At this, the heroic grandsire [Drona], the grand old man of the Kurus, gave a loud lion's roar and blew his conch to hearten Duryodhana.

(13) Thereupon, conches, drums, cymbals and trumpets were sounded all at once. Terrific was the noise.

(14) Then Madhava [Krishna] and Pandava [Arjuna], standing in their great chariot yoked with white steeds, blew their divine conches.

(15) Hrishikesha [Krishna] blew the Panchajanya and Dhananjaya [Arjuna] the Devadatta, while the wolf-bellied Bhima of dread deeds sounded his great conch Paundra.

(16) King Yudhishthira, Kunti's son, blew the Anantavijaya, and Nakula and Sahadeva their conches, Sughosha and Manipushpaka.

(17) And Kashiraja, the great bowman, Shikhandi the *maharatha*, Dhrishtadyumna, Virata and Satyaki, the unconquerable,

(18) Drupada, Draupadi's son, and the strong-armed son of the Subhadra — all these, O King, blew each his own conch.

(19) That terrifying tumult, causing earth and heaven to resound, rent the hearts of Dhritarashtra's sons.

(20) Then, O King, the ape-bannered Pandava [Arjuna], seeing Dhritarashtra's sons arrayed and flight of arrows about to begin, took up his bow,

---

(21) And spoke thus to Hrishikesha [Krishna]: Set my chariot between the two armies, O Achyuta!

(22) That I may behold them drawn up on battle intent, and know whom I have to engage in this fearful combat,

(23) And that I may survey the fighters assembled here, anxious to fulfill in battle perverse Duryodhana's desire.

Arjuna is asking here not whether it is necessary that he should fight, but against whom he has to fight. If he did not wish to fight, he would have told Krishna so on the previous day itself. He had no aversion to fighting as such. He was always prepared to fight.

(24) Thus addressed by Gudakesha, O King, Hrishikesha set the unique chariot between the two armies,

(25) In front of Bhishma, Drona and all the Kings and said: Behold, O Partha, the Kurus assembled yonder.

(26) Then did Partha see, standing there, sires, grandsires, preceptors, uncles, brothers, sons, grandsons, comrades,

(27) Fathers-in-law, and friends in both armies. Beholding all these kinsmen ranged before him, Kaunteya was overcome with great compassion and spake thus in anguish:

Arjuna Said:

(28) As I look upon these kinsmen, O Krishna, assembled here eager to fight,

(29) My limbs fail, my mouth is parched, a tremor shakes my frame and my hair stands on end.

---

(30) Gandiva [Arjuna's bow] slips from my hand, my skin is on fire, I cannot keep my feet, and my mind reels.

(31) I have unhappy forebodings, O Keshava, and I see no good in slaying kinsmen in battle.

He sees that all of them are relatives and friends, whom one cannot easily bring oneself to kill. Arjuna says, "I do not see any good in killing one's kinsmen" The stress here is on "kinsmen."

(32) I seek not victory, nor sovereign power, nor earthly joys. What good are sovereign power, worldly pleasures and even life to us, O Govinda?

(33) Those for whom we would desire sovereign power, earthly joys and delights are here arrayed in battle, having renounced life and wealth —

(34) Preceptors, sires, grandsires, sons and even grand-sons, uncles, fathers-in-law, brothers-in-law, and other kins-men.

(35) These I would not kill, O Madhusudana, even though they slay me, not even for kingship of the three worlds, much less for an earthly kingdom.

(36) What pleasure can there be in slaying these sons of Dhritarashtra, O Janardana? Sin only can be our lot if we slay these, usurpers though they be.

(37) It does not therefore behoove us to kill our kinsmen, these sons of Dhritarashtra. How may we be happy, O Madhava, in killing our own kin?

(38) Even though these, their wits warped by greed, see not the guilt that lies in destroying the family, nor the sin of treachery to comrades,

(39) How can we, O Janardana, help recoiling from this sin, seeing clearly as we do the guilt that lies in such destruction?

He is unhappy not at the thought of killing, but at the thought of whom he was required to kill. By putting the word "kinsmen" repeatedly in his mouth, the author of the Gita shows into what darkness and ignorance he has sunk. Arjuna has been arguing from a practical point of view and Shri Krishna will try to answer that argument.

(40) With the destruction of the family perish the eternal family virtues, and with the perishing of these virtues unrighteousness seizes the whole family.

(41) When unrighteousness prevails, O Krishna, the women of the family become corrupt, and their corruption, O Varshneya, causes a confusion of *varnas* [social classes].

(42) This confusion verily drags the family-slayer, as well as the family, to hell, and for want of obsequial offerings and rites their departed sires fall from blessedness.

(43) By the sins of these family-slayers, resulting in the confusion of *varnas*, the eternal tribal and family virtues are brought to naught;

(44) For we have had it handed down to us, O Janardana, that the men whose family virtues have been ruined are doomed to dwell in hell.

---

(45) Alas! What a heinous sin we are about to commit, in that, from greed of the joy of sovereign power, we are prepared to slay our kith and kin!

(46) Happier far would it be for me if Dhritarashtra's sons, weapons in hand, should strike me down on the battlefield, unresisting and unarmed.

(47) Thus spake Arjuna on the field of battle and, dropping his bow and arrows, sank down on his seat in the chariot, overwhelmed with anguish.

If we see anyone, here or elsewhere, who renounces a fight in regard to worldly matters and forgives even strangers, not to speak of relations, we should think of him as a good man. If we desist from beating up a thief or any other felon and do nothing to get him punished but, after admonishing him and recovering from him the stolen article, let him go, we would be credited with humanity and our action would be regarded as an instance of nonviolence. A contrary course would be looked upon as violence. How is it, then, that Shri Krishna stops Arjuna from advancing such an argument? How can we explain a plainly contrary teaching in the Bhagavad Gita? Why does Shri Krishna describe Arjuna as cowardly and weak?

The Bhagavad Gita is consistent from the first to the last verse. That is why we meditate on its teaching and hope to discover from it the path to *moksha*. We should, therefore, think whether Arjuna's argument is valid or contains some flaw.

It is important to consider what Arjuna's question was and what the circumstances were in which he raised it. Having got his chariot stationed between the two armies, he said he wanted to see who those men were against whom he would be fighting.

His reason is, for the time being, clouded. He has lost his nerve. All that has come before shows that Arjuna is a great warrior and that, when starting out to fight, he does not hesitate and ask all manner of questions. In the past, he never hesitated even when he had to fight against relations. What is more, victory in the battle depends entirely on him. In their preparations for the battle during fourteen years' exile, the other brothers always placed Arjuna at their head.

Let us suppose that Arjuna flees the battlefield. Though his enemies are wicked people, are sinners, they are his relations and he cannot bring himself to kill them. If he leaves the field, what would happen to those vast numbers on his side? If Arjuna went away, leaving them behind, would the Kauravas have mercy on them? No. If he left the battle, the Pandava army would be simply annihilated. What, then, would be the plight of their wives and children?

If Arjuna had left the battlefield, the very calamities which he feared would have befallen them. Their families would have been ruined, and the traditional *dharma* of these families and the race would have been destroyed. Arjuna, therefore, had no choice but to fight.

This is the meaning of the battle in crude physical terms. I shall discuss later what it would be if the battlefield were taken to be the human being.

Chapter Two

By reason of delusion, man takes wrong to be right. By reason of delusion was Arjuna led to make a distinction between kinsmen and nonkinsmen. To demonstrate that this is a vain distinction, Lord Krishna distinguishes between body (not-self) and *Atman* (Self) and shows that while bodies are impermanent and several, *Atman* is permanent and one.

(1) To Arjuna, thus overcome with compassion, sorrowing, and his eyes obscured by flowing tears, Madhusudana spoke these words:

The Lord said:

(2) How is it that this perilous moment, this delusion, unworthy of the noble, leading neither to heaven nor to glory, has overtaken thee?

(3) Yield not to unmanliness, O Partha. It does not become thee. Shake off this miserable faint-heartedness and arise, O Parantapa.

Arjuna Said:

(4) How shall I, with arrows, engage Bhishma and Drona in battle, O Madhusudana, they who are worthy of reverence, O Arisudana?

(5) It were better far to live on alms in this world than to slay these venerable elders. Having slain them I should but have blood-stained enjoyments.

(6) Nor do we know which is better for us, that we conquer them or that they conquer us; for here stand before us Dhritarashtra's sons, having killed whom we should have no desire to live.

(7) My being is paralyzed by faint-heartedness. My mind discerns not duty. Hence I ask thee — tell me, I pray thee, in no uncertain language — wherein lies my good? I am thy disciple. Guide me. I seek refuge in thee.

(8) For I see nothing that can dispel the anguish that shrivels up my senses, even if I should win on earth uncontested sovereignty over a thriving kingdom or lordship over the gods.

(9) Thus spoke Gudakesha Parantapa to Hrishikesha Govinda, and, with the words "I will not fight", became speechless.

The author has used the word Gudakesha for Arjuna. It means one who has conquered sleep, who is always vigilant. We should, therefore, think carefully about this illustration of the battle. The first thing to bear in mind is that Arjuna falls into the error of making a distinction between kinsmen and outsiders. Outsiders may be killed even if they are not oppressors, and kinsmen may not be killed even if they are.

The Gita says, "No, this is not right. We have no right to point an accusing finger at others. We should point out the lapses of our own people first." Should it become necessary to cut off, with a sword, one's father's head, one must do so if one has a sword and is a Kshatriya [member of the warrior caste], and if one would be ready to cut off anyone else's head in similar circumstances. Shri Krishna, therefore, asks Arjuna to free himself from ignorant attachment in this world.

How should I act as editor of *Navajivan* [Gandhi's weekly publication]? Would it be right for me to proclaim with beat of drum the theft committed by an outsider's child and say nothing about a boy of my ashram who may have misbehaved in the same way? Certainly not. The Gita permits no distinction between one's relations and others.

Even if we believe in nonviolence, it would not be proper for us to refuse, through cowardice, to protect the weak. If Arjuna had forgotten the difference between kinsmen and others, and had been so filled with the spirit of nonviolence as to bring about a change of heart in Duryodhana, he would have been another Shri Krishna. Actually, however, he believed Duryodhana to be wicked. I might be ready to embrace a snake, but, if one comes to bite you, I should kill it and protect you.

Arjuna has two courses open to him: he should either kill Duryodhana and others, or else convert them. In the circumstances, Arjuna's laying down arms would mean the annihilation of all those on his side. His refusal to fight would bring on a disaster.

(10) To him thus stricken with anguish, O Bharata, between the two armies, Hrishikesha, as though mocking, addressed these words:

From today we begin the argument of the Gita and shall not, therefore, be able to go as fast with the verses as we have been doing.

The argument addressed to Arjuna begins with the eleventh verse, and continues right up to the last chapter. Shri Krishna starts with the distinction between the *Atman* and the body, for that is the first step to spiritual knowledge. We must first know certain definitions, then alone can we proceed. Arjuna is represented as a seeker, and so Shri Krishna starts giving him the knowledge of the *Atman*. One becomes entitled to ask questions and seek illumination only if one has observed control of the senses and always followed Truth, and only then will one's questions deserve to be answered. Arjuna has this fitness. He has the genuine spirit of submission and humility.

The Lord said:

(11) Thou mournest for them whom thou shouldst not mourn, and utterest vain words of wisdom. The wise mourn neither for the living nor for the dead.

(12) For never was I not, nor thou nor these kings, nor will any of us cease to be hereafter.

(13) As the embodied one has, in the present body, infancy, youth, age, even so does he receive another body. The wise man is not deceived therein.

Shri Krishna tells Arjuna that he is talking specious wisdom. The Gita does not teach the path of action, nor of knowledge, nor of devotion. No matter how diligent one is in performing good actions or what measure of *bhakti* [devotion] one practices, one can attain self-realization only if one sheds his attachment to the ego. It is possible only for a person who has succeeded in doing so.

A man's devotion to God is to be judged from the extent to which he gives up his stiffness and bends low in humility. Only then will he be, not an impostor, but a truly illumined man, a man of genuine knowledge. The Gita, then, does not advocate any one of the three paths [action, knowledge or devotion]. I have from my experience come to the conclusion that it has ·been composed to teach this one truth which I have explained: we can follow truth only in the measure that we shed our attachment to the ego. It is to teach this that Shri Krishna has advanced the beautiful argument of the Gita.

(14) O Kaunteya, contacts of the senses with their objects bring cold and heat, pleasure and pain. They come and go and are transient. Endure them, O Bharata.

(15) O noblest of men, the wise man who is not disturbed or agitated by these, who is unmoved by pleasure and pain, he alone is fitted for immortality.

Any being who is not subject to the impressions of senses will never experience fear. It is these impressions which are responsible for the feelings of happiness and misery. Someone has said that the muscles of a man who is angry become thirteen times as tense as when he is normal, and of a man who is laughing nine times as tense. That is, one spends more energy when one is angry, and one whose energy is thus wasted cannot attain to immortality. The cultivation of this state [non-attachment to sense perceptions] requires practice. We can even say of a person who has attained to it that he is God.

During the early days of my legal practice, I was on one occasion very much troubled in my mind. I then went out for a walk. I was very much agitated. I then remembered this verse, and the very next moment I was almost dancing with relief. We should identify ourselves with Arjuna and have faith that Shri Krishna is driving our chariot.

This Krishna is not the person who, when the hour of his death arrived, fell to a hunter's arrow, and Arjuna is not that person from whose hand the Gandiva bow slipped. Krishna is the *Atman* in us, who is our charioteer. We can win only if we hand over the reins of the chariot to him. God makes us dance, like the master in a puppet show. We are smaller than even puppets. We should, therefore, trust everything to God, as children to parents. Let us not eat uncooked stuff. Let Krishna the cook prepare and give us the food of grace. He wills for our *Atman*.

(16) What is Non-Being is never known to have been, and what is Being is never known not to have been. Of both these the secret has been seen by the seers of the Truth.

The *jnanis*, the men of knowledge, have discovered what exists and what does not exist. Name and form are brittle as glass. The *jnanis* know what is implied in the difference between existence and nonexistence. We only know one simple thing: God is, nothing else is.

(17) Know that to be imperishable whereby all this is pervaded. No one can destroy that immutable Being.

(18) These bodies of the embodied one who is eternal, imperishable and immeasurable are finite. Fight, therefore, O Bharata.

If we argue that since all bodies are perishable, one may kill, does it follow that I may kill all the women and children in the ashram? Would I have, in doing so, acted according to the teaching of the Bhagavad Gita, merely because their bodies are perishable? We believe the watchman to have been mad because he killed a person. If, however, he were to cite this verse of the Gita to justify what he did, we would call him wicked. What, then, shall we say of a person who mouths these seemingly learned arguments and then commits wickedness? To know the answer to this, we should go back to the first chapter. Arjuna said that he did not want even the kingdom of gods if he had to kill his kith and kin for that; but he is bound, in any case, to kill them, for he has accepted the *dharma* which requires him to kill. Verse 18 applies to him, but it does not apply to others.

(19) He who thinks of This (*Atman*) as slayer and he who believes This to be slain, are both ignorant. This neither slays nor is ever slain.

(20) This is never born nor ever dies, nor having been will ever not be any more — unborn, eternal, everlasting, ancient. This is not slain when the body is slain.

(21) He who knows This, O Partha, to be imperishable, eternal, unborn and immutable — whom and how can that man slay or cause to be slain?

(22) As a man casts off worn-out garments and takes others that are new, even so the embodied one casts off worn-out bodies and passes on to others new.

(23) This no weapons wound. This no fire burns. This no waters wet. This no wind doth dry.

---

(24) Beyond all cutting, burning, wetting and drying is This
— eternal, all-pervading, stable, immovable, everlasting,

(25) Perceivable neither by the senses nor by the mind.
This is called unchangeable. Therefore, knowing This as
such, thou shouldst not grieve.

Having argued thus, Shri Krishna says, "But suppose that
the *Atman* has none of these attributes. What of it? What even
if it is born and dies again and again? All the more reason why
you should not grieve over death."

(26) And if thou deemest This to be always coming to
birth and always dying, even then, O Mahabahu, thou
shouldst not grieve;

(27) For certain is the death of the born, and certain is
the birth of the dead. Therefore, what is unavoidable thou
shouldst not regret.

(28) The state of all beings before birth is unmanifest.
Their middle state is manifest. Their state after death is again
unmanifest. What occasion is there for lament, O Bharata?

Why, then, grieve? This is the great mystery of God. As a
magician creates the illusion of a tree and destroys it, so God
sports in endless ways and does not let us know the beginning
and the end of his play. Why grieve over this?

(29) One looks upon This is a marvel. Another speaks of
This as such. Another hears thereof as a marvel; yet, having heard of This, none truly knows This.

(30) This embodied one in the body of every being is ever beyond all harm, O Bharata; Thou shouldst not, therefore, grieve for anyone.

Thus far Lord Krishna, by force of argument based upon pure reason, has demonstrated that *Atman* is abiding while the physical body is fleeting, and has explained that if, under certain circumstances, the destruction of a physical body is deemed justifiable, it is delusion to imagine that the Kauravas should not be slain because they are kinsmen. Now he reminds Arjuna of the duty of a Kshatriya.

(31) Again, seeing thine own duty thou shouldst not shrink from it, for there is no higher good for a Kshatriya than a righteous war.

(32) Such a fight, coming unsought, as a gateway to heaven thrown open, falls only to the lot of happy Kshatriyas, O Partha.

(33) But if thou wilt not fight this righteous fight, then failing in thy duty and losing thine honor thou wilt incur sin.

(34) The world will forever recount the story of thy disgrace, and for a man of honor disgrace is worse than death.

(35) The great warriors will think that fear made thee retire from battle, and thou wilt fail in the esteem of those very ones who have held thee high.

(36) Thine enemies will deride thy prowess and speak many unspeakable words about thee. What can be more painful than that?

---

(37) Slain, thou shalt gain heaven. Victorious, thou shalt inherit the earth. Therefore arise, O Kaunteya, determined to fight.

Having declared the highest truth — the immortality of the eternal *Atman* and the fleeting nature of the physical body (11-30) — Krishna reminds Arjuna that a Kshatriya may not flinch from a fight which comes unsought (31-32). He then (33-37) shows how the highest truth and the performance of duty incidentally coincide with expediency. Next he proceeds to foreshadow the central teaching of the Gita in the following verse.

(38) Hold alike pleasure and pain, gain and loss, victory and defeat, and gird up thy loins for the fight. So doing thou shalt not incur sin.

(39) Thus have I set before thee the attitude of knowledge [*Sankhya*]. Bear now the attitude of action [*yoga*]. Resorting to this attitude thou shalt cast off the bondage of action.

The word *Sankhya*, it has been said, is somewhat confusing. It may be so for the learned, it is not so for us. All that Shri Krishna means is this: "I explained the matter to you from a theoretical point of view. I pointed out the difference between the *Atman* and the body. Having explained this to you, I will now put the argument with reference to *yoga*. *Yoga* means practice. After understanding this, you will have to translate your knowledge into action in the manner I shall explain." The word *yoga* is used repeatedly in the Gita. It explains how to act. "If you understand this," Shri Krishna says, "You will escape from the bondage of action."

(40) Here no effort undertaken is lost, no disaster befalls. Even a little of this righteous course delivers one from great fear.

No sin is incurred by those that follow the path of action. A beginning made is not wasted. Even a little effort along this path saves one from great danger. This is a royal road, easy to follow. It is the sovereign *yoga*. In following it, there is no fear of stumbling. Once a beginning is made, nothing will stand in our way.

This is a very important verse. It contains the profound idea that nothing done is ever lost, that there is no sin in the path of action. This is the royal road. This path is the path of Truth. There is no harm, no fear of destruction, in following it.

(41) The attitude in this matter, springing, as it does, from fixed resolve is but one, O Kurunandana; but for those who have no fixed resolve the attitudes are many-branched and unending.

The resolute intellect here is one-pointed. Along this path one must hold one's intellect so firm that there is no wavering. The actions of a man whose intellect is not fixed on one aim, who is not single-minded in his devotion, will branch out in many directions. As the mind leaps, monkey-fashion, from branch to branch, so will the intellect.

In present-day politics, there is no good at all and plenty of evil, for it is full of flattery and one is not protected from dangers, but, on the contrary, surrounded by them. It does not help us to realize the *Atman*. In fact we lose our soul. We lose our *dharma*, we lose the capacity for good works, lose both this world and the other.

If, on the other hand, we can have faith in this spinning-wheel movement [Gandhi's independence movement, based, in part, on reviving village industries such as handspinning and handweaving], we can serve the world, be happy ourselves, can live safe from a great danger, that is, can live without fear of those who would hold us down. We also secure, simultaneously, a means of ensuring our welfare in the other world. If a person who takes up this work does not seem to be of a fixed mind, you may conclude that he is not following the royal path.

(42-44) The ignorant, reveling in the letter of the Vedas, declare that there is naught else. Carnally-minded, holding heaven to be their goal, they utter swelling words which promise birth as the fruit of action, and which dwell on the many and varied rites to be performed for the sake of pleasure and power. Intent as they are on pleasure and power, their swelling words rob them of their wits, and they have no settled attitude which can be centered on the supreme goal.

The Vedic ritual, as opposed to the doctrine of *yoga* laid down in the Gita, is alluded to here. The Vedic ritual lays down countless ceremonies and rites with a view to attaining merit and heaven. These, divorced as they are from the essence of the Vedas and short-lived in their result, are worthless.

I was once asked by someone why I had not succeeded in realizing the *Atman*. I told him that for me the means themselves stood for such realization. The fact that such a question was asked is enough to suggest that the person who put it would not understand the humility which inspired my reply.

The mind of a person who, addressed as "*Mahatma*" [Great

Soul] this day, hopes to be so addressed ever afterwards — the mind of such a person is distracted by all manner of thoughts and attractive visions. His mind will not be plain white, like *khadi* [handspun, handwoven cloth]. He is ever wanting to dress his mind, as fashionable women do their bodies, in many-colored saris with borders of various designs.

Such a person can never be devoted to God. Only he who has a spirit of extreme humility can be said to have a resolute intellect.

(45) The Vedas have as their domain the three *gunas*. Eschew them, O Arjuna. Free thyself from the pairs of opposites. Abide in eternal truth. Scorn to gain or guard anything. Remain the master of the soul.

Shri Krishna is here talking about the Vedas as expounded by the ritualist pedants. His statement, "Eschew them", therefore, gives only one side of the truth. The Vedas which utter *"Neti, neti"*["Not this, not this."] — there is nothing except Truth — those Vedas are ever the objects of reverence for us. We can cite verses, from the Gita itself that tell us to accept the Vedas as thus understood.

(46) To the extent that a well is of use when there is a flood of water on all sides, to the same extent are all the Vedas of use to an enlightened Brahmin.

What may be found in a tank will also be found in a big lake. He who knows *Brahman* will know everything else. He who has reached the Gangotri [a tributary of the Ganges] has known the Ganges. We get from the former all the benefit we would from the latter. Some interpret this verse in a different way, but we shall not go into that.

(47) Action alone is the province, never the fruits thereof. Let not thy motive be the fruit of action, nor shouldst thou desire to avoid action.

Your right is to work, and not to expect the fruit. The slave-owner tells the slave, "Mind your work, but beware lest you pluck a fruit from the garden. Yours is to take what I give." God has put us under restriction in the same manner. He tells us that we may work if we wish, but that the reward of work is entirely for Him to give.

The eyelids certainly protect the eyes, but they do not do so with conscious intention. They protect the eyes by reflex action. The relationship between God and man is similarly spontaneous. Mirabai has sung, "By a slender thread has Hari tied me to Him, and I turn as He pulls the thread." The relationship between us and God is of the kind described here. The thread is slender, and a single one besides.

(48) Act thou, O Dhananjaya, without attachment, steadfast in *yoga*, even-minded in success and failure. Even-mindedness is *yoga*. Work without attachment, being established firmly in *yoga*;

We should do no work with attachment. Attachment to good work, is that too wrong? Yes, it is. If we are attached to our goal of winning liberty, we shall not hesitate to adopt bad means. If a person is particular that he would give coins to me personally, one day he might even steal them. Hence, we should not be attached even to a good cause. Only then will our means remain pure and our actions, too.

(49) For action, O Dhananjaya, is far inferior to unattached action. Seek refuge in the attitude of detachment. Pitiable are those who make fruit their motive.

(50) Here in this world a man gifted with that attitude of detachment escapes the fruit of both good and evil deed. Gird thyself up for *yoga*, therefore. *Yoga* is skill in action.

Yoga means nothing but skill in work. Anyone who wants to decide whether he should or should not do a particular thing, should seek a *yogi's* advice. This is why it is said that where there is a prince of *yogis* like Shri Krishna and a bowman of prowess like Arjuna, prosperity and power follow as a matter of course.

(51) For sages, gifted with the attitude of detachment, who renounce the fruit of action, are released from the bondage of birth and attain to the state which is free from all ills.

(52) When thy understanding will have passed through the slough of delusion, then wilt thou be indifferent alike to what thou hast heard and wilt hear.

(53) When thy understanding, distracted by much hearing, will rest steadfast and unmoved in concentration, then wilt thou attain *yoga*.

When your intellect, once perverted by listening to all manner of arguments, is totally absorbed in the contemplation of

God, you will then attain to *yoga*. When a person is firmly estab-lished in *samadhi* he is filled with ecstatic love and, therefore, can be completely indifferent to this world.

Arjuna said:

(54) What, O Keshava, is the mark of the man whose understanding is secure, whose mind is fixed in concentra-tion? How does he talk? How sit? How move?

The food which the Gita offers is different from what one's mother gives. Before Mother Gita, the earthly mother stands no comparison. He who has the Gita always engraved in his heart and keeps it there till the moment of death, will attain to *moksha*. We recite the following [eighteen] verses daily so that we may understand their meaning and be guided by them.

The Lord said:

(55) When a man puts away, O Partha, all the cravings that arise in the mind and finds comfort for himself only from *Atman*, then is he called the man of secure under-standing.

To find comfort for oneself from *Atman* means to look to the spirit within for spiritual comfort, not to outside objects, which in their very nature must give pleasure as well as pain. Spiritual comfort or bliss must be distinguished from pleasure or happiness. The pleasure I may derive from the possession of wealth, for instance, is delusive. Real spiritual comfort or bliss can be attained only if I rise superior to every temptation, even though troubled by the pangs of poverty and hunger.

Anyone who wants to live in such a state must give up everything which is likely to obstruct his effort. If all that we do is merely to indulge in fancies, it would be better not to think at all, neither good thoughts nor bad. The road to hell is paved with good intentions. That is why it is said that one may cast into a river a ton of thoughts and cling to an ounce of practice.

(56) Whose mind is untroubled in sorrows and longeth not for joys, who is free from passion, fear and wrath — he is called the ascetic of secure understanding.

(57) Who owns attachment nowhere, who feels neither joy nor resentment whether good or bad comes his way — that man's understanding is secure.

(58) And when, like the tortoise drawing in its limbs from every side, this man draws in his senses from their objects, his understanding is secure.

Only that man who voluntarily holds in his senses may be known as completely absorbed in God. When our senses seem to move out of our control, we should think of the tortoise. The objects of the senses are like pebbles. If we hold in the senses, the pebbles will not hurt, that is, if we hold under control our hands, our feet, our eyes, and so on.

(59) When a man starves his senses, the objects of those senses disappear from him, but not the yearning for them. The yearning too departs when he beholds the Supreme.

The purport of this verse is that we should fast for self-purification; but the *shastras* tell us that, while fasting, we should wish with all our strength for freedom from desire. If, in addition, we also yearn to see God, then only will our fasting bear fruit. If we desire that our appetite should subside, it is in order that we may see God.

When we are fasting, our one desire should be to see God. Our appetites stand in the way, and so we must weaken their hold on us. After a person has seen God, it is all one to him whether he eats or does not eat. Vinoba tells a story about Chaitanya, that a lump of sugar placed on his tongue remained there undissolved, like a stone. The reason for this was that his pleasure in objects of sense had completely died away.

Chaitanyadeva felt all the time that it was God's grace which sustained him and that if he should eat at all, it must be only that he may see God one day. To see Him, one should completely conquer one's appetites, and even the instinctive pleasure one feels in objects of sense must subside. This verse provides the key to such a state.

This is a very important verse. Four or five hundred years ago, in Europe and Arabia they attached great importance to mortification of the flesh. In the time of the Prophet [Mohammed], prayer, fasting and keeping awake at night were considered essential for subduing the *nafar* (this is a very good word denoting the sense-organs collectively. It also means desire). The Prophet was often awake till two or three after midnight, and was never particular when and what he ate. To the Prophet, fasting brought happiness, for it was an occasion when he could live constantly in the presence of God.

Jesus did likewise. He lived in solitude, fasted for forty days and subjected his body to the utmost mortification. At the end of forty days, he felt that he heard a mysterious voice, that

God was talking to him and that the veil which hid God from him had lifted. Those who followed him taught the same thing. There has been a tradition of fasting and prayer in Europe right to the present day.

And then came Luther in Germany. He said that the others had misinterpreted the text, and that their lives were all deception. He plainly saw the superstitions and hypocrisies which flourished in monasteries. Those who believed in mortifying the flesh thought it their duty to curb the senses and to kill others who did not do so. Observing these evils, Luther went to the opposite extreme. The Protestants believed that there was nothing but hypocrisy in the Catholic practices, and so they destroyed [the practice of fasting], a most potent means of realizing God.

Because this means harmed some people, it does not follow that it harms all. If anyone is convinced that he ought to kill his physical appetites, he does nothing wrong in fasting. If he has faith, it will certainly be rewarded.

(60) For, in spite of the wise man's endeavour, O Kaunteya, the unruly senses distract his mind perforce.

If the rider is not vigilant and the reins are not all tight, there is no knowing where they will carry him. "A monkey, and drunk besides," that is how it will be.

(61) Holding all these in check, the *yogi* should sit intent on Me; for he whose senses are under control is secure of understanding.

I explained yesterday that, in order that our pleasure in the objects of senses may subside completely, fasting, devotion, prayer and vigils are necessary; but the pleasure in objects will not disappear till we have realized God. The question is, can it disappear completely while the body is there? I have come to the conclusion that no one can be called *mukta* [liberated] while he is still alive. One may be said at the most to have become fit for *moksha*.

It is doing violence to the meaning of words to say that a man has attained deliverance even while he lives in the body, for the necessity for deliverance remains so long as connection with the body remains. A little reflection will show us that, if our egoistic attachment to ourselves has completely disappeared, the body cannot survive. If we have no wish at all to keep the body alive, it must cease to exist. If we but move our hand the mind is bound to move, too. If, now, we would completely withdraw the mind from the body, the latter should become "as the burnt silken thread, only the form surviving."

Some attachment is bound to persist while our bodies are capable of motion. Scientists remove air from a bottle, but a little of it remains in it. The air becomes more and more rarefied, and only a scientist would know that there was any inside. Similarly, our pleasure in objects does not disappear completely while the least degree of association with the body persists, as signified by its movements.

Thus, the cravings of the senses die away only when we cease to exist in the body. This is a terrible statement to make, but the Gita does not shrink from stating terrible truths.

We need not spend much thought or indulge in intellectual exercises over this problem. Once we are decided on the end, we should concentrate our attention on the means. If they are right, the end is as good as attained.

(62) In a man brooding on objects of the senses, attachment to them springs up. Attachment begets craving and craving begets wrath.

(63) Wrath breeds stupefaction, stupefaction leads to loss of memory, loss of memory ruins the reason, and the ruin of reason spells utter destruction;

(64) But the disciplined soul, moving among sense-objects with the senses weaned from likes and dislikes and brought under the control of *Atman*, attains peace of mind.

He who lives with his senses no longer subject to attachments and aversions and perfectly under his control becomes fit for God's grace.

(65) Peace of mind means the end of all ills; for the understanding of him whose mind is at peace stands secure.

When God's grace descends on us, bringing us peace, all our suffering ends. Who can harm him who is protected by Rama [God]? He on whom God showers His grace has all his sufferings destroyed.

(66) The undisciplined man has neither understanding nor devotion; for, for him who has no devotion, there is no peace, and for him who has no peace whence happiness?

(67) For when his mind turns after any of the roaming senses, it sweeps away his understanding, as the wind a vessel upon the waters.

---

(68) Therefore, O Mahabahu, he whose senses are reined in on all sides from their objects is the man of secure understanding.

(69) When it is night for all other beings, the disciplined soul is awake. When all other beings are awake, it is night for the seeing ascetic.

In conclusion, Shri Krishna gives the mark of a *sthitaprajna* [a person of steadfast wisdom] in one verse. He is awake when it is night for other human beings, and when other human beings and all the creatures seem to be awake, it is night for the ascetic who sees.

This should be the ideal for the Satyagraha Ashram. Let us pray that we may see light when all around us there is darkness. If we are brave, the whole world will be brave. As in our body, so in the universe — this is how we should feel. We should thus be ready to take upon ourselves the burden of the whole world; but we can bear the burden only if we mean by it doing voluntary suffering on behalf of the entire world. We shall then see light where others see nothing but darkness. Let others think that the spinning wheel is useless, and believe that we cannot win liberty by keeping fasts. We should tell them that we are sure we shall get it.

The world will tell us that the senses cannot be controlled. We should reply that they certainly can be. If people tell us that Truth does not avail in the world, we should reply that it does. The world and the man established in *samadhi* are like the west and the east. The world's night is our day and the world's day is our night. There is, thus, noncooperation between the two. This should be our attitude if we understand the Gita rightly. This does not mean that we are superior to others. We are humble men and women. We are a mere drop while the world is the ocean; but we should have the faith that, if we succeed in crossing to the other shore, the world, too, will.

Yesterday we learned an important mark of the *sthitaprajna*. What seems light to other people is darkness to the *yogi*. For instance, we tell a great number of people that they should eat sparingly, but a man who has spent his days in devotion to God will immediately understand that if he eats full meals every day, it will be a hindrance to his life of devotion. Such a *yogi*, therefore, will keep himself alive on very little food while other people go on feasting on delicacies.

But he will not parade his self-control. Narasinha Mehta ridiculed in his song renunciation, knowledge, meditation, etc., and gave the palm to the *gopi's* [the playful milkmaids who loved the young Krishna] love; but this sounds strange to people in the modern age. The truth is that those whom the world knows as *yogis* are not really *yogis*, nor is what the world describes as "spiritual enlightenment" such in fact. This phrase is used merely to deceive the world. The man who really lives a life of contemplation will outwardly seem a man of the world. His mind may be absorbed in God all the hours of the day, but he will move in the world like other men. He will not go about trumpeting that he lives a life of contemplation. The *gopis* in their love go on dancing; for, knowing that their love is pure, they are not afraid of the world's censure.

(70) He in whom all longings subside, even as the waters subside in the ocean which, though ever being filled by them, never overflows — that man finds peace, not he who cherishes longing.

(71) The man who sheds all longing and moves without concern, free from the sense of "I" and "mine" — he attains peace.

(72) This is the state, O Partha, of the man who rests in *Brahman*. Having attained to it, he is not deluded. He who abides in this state even at the hour of death passes into oneness with *Brahman*.

If a man who has lived a wicked life till now takes to a good life from tomorrow, there is nothing he will lack; but it will not avail a man to have been good all his life if in his last days he becomes wicked. That man, then, may be said to be good who remains so till the last day of his life. That is why it is said, "Call no man good till he is dead." However good a man may have been, he may yet weaken in his old age and worry over his children and his social affairs. We may know that a man has attained *moksha* only if he died in the *brahmi* state.

The *nirvana* of the Buddhists is *shunyata*, emptiness, but the *nirvana* of the Gita means peace and that is why it is described as *brahma-nirvana* [oneness with *Brahman*]. We need not concern ourselves with this distinction. There is no reason for supposing that there is a difference between the *nirvana* mentioned by Lord Buddha and the *nirvana* of the Gita. Buddha's description of *nirvana* and this other description of *nirvana* refer to the same state. A number of learned men have shown that the Buddha did not teach a doctrine denying the existence of God; but all these are pointless controversies. What can we say about a state which is so different from anything known in our life that we cannot describe it even when we have attained to it? If it is agreed that our bodily existence is not a thing to be cherished, all these other controversies are un-meaning.

———

Chapter Three

The chapter which we completed yesterday is known as *Sankhya Yoga*. We saw that, after discussing the distinction between the body and the *Atman*, Shri Krishna told Arjuna that he had explained the *Sankhya* view, that is, analyzed logically the distinction between the body and the *Atman*. This did not help Arjuna to know it in his own experience, but he grasped it intellectually. Arjuna's duty of fighting was explained to him, but only so far as it could be done with the help of argument. Shri Krishna then explained *yoga* to him, that is, the method of acting in a disinterested spirit. This led to the discussion concerning the man of steadfast wisdom.

From the last verse of chapter two, it would seem that Shri Krishna had nothing further to add. Indeed, if Arjuna had not again put a question to him, there was really nothing for him to add; but in view of the natural tendency in everyone to let his desires rule his reason, truth has to be repeated often so that it may be made more clear. If an unenlightened man decides for himself, he usually decides in favor of worldliness. Therefore, he has to keep on repeating to himself that he is the *Atman*, for it is not a truth experienced by him at all hours of the day.

Vyasa has placed before readers a divine truth through the Gita. Whether *Sankhya* or *yoga*, *sannyasa* or the life of the householder, all these paths are essentially one. Action and inaction mean the same thing, this is the substance of the Gita's teaching. Since these different paths are so mixed up with one another, we should understand their essential identity if our one aim is to know God and realize the unreality of all else. The way to know Him is not to sit cross-legged, but to work in a disinterested spirit.

A man does not become a *yogi* because he is known to have performed a thousand *yajnas* [sacrifices] or made huge gifts. We have to take into account whether he was free from attachment to the ego, whether he willingly turned (in Mira's words) as God pulled him with a slender thread, whether he worked accordingly, and so on. Vyasa wants to tell us that a *yogi* should offer up to God everything he does, whether it be good or indifferent, should look upon Him as the sole author of everything. And so he makes Arjuna ask Krishna:

Arjuna said:

(1) If, O Janardana, thou holdest that the attitude of detachment is superior to action, then why, O Keshava, dost thou urge me to dreadful action?

(2) Thou dost seem to confuse my understanding with perplexing speech. Tell me, therefore, in no uncertain voice, that alone whereby I may attain salvation.

Arjuna is sore perplexed, for while on the one hand he is rebuked for his faintheartedness, on the other he seems to be advised to refrain from action; but this, in reality, is not the case, as the following verses will show.

The Lord said:

(3) I have spoken before, O sinless one, of two attitudes in this world: the *Sankhya's*, that of the *Yoga* of Knowledge; and the *Yogi's*, that of *karma yoga*.

(4) Never does man enjoy freedom from action by not undertaking action, nor does he attain that freedom by mere renunciation of action.

"Freedom from action" is freedom from the bondage of action. This freedom is not to be gained from cessation of all activity, apart from the fact that this cessation is in the very nature of things impossible (see the following verse). How then may it be gained? The following *shlokas* will explain.

(5) For none ever remains inactive even for a moment; for all are compelled to action by the *gunas* inherent in *prakriti*.

No one can cease from *karma* [action] even for a moment. To listen and not to listen, both are forms of *karma*. *Sattva, rajas* and *tamas*, the three forces or modes [*gunas*] of *prakriti* [nature], drive everyone to action, whether he will or no. A *tamasic* man is one who works in a mechanical fashion; a *rajasic* man is one who rides too many horses, who is restless and is always doing something or other; and the *sattvic* man is one who works with peace in his mind. One is always driven to work by one or another of these three modes of *prakriti* or by a combination of them.

(6) He who curbs the organs of action but allows the mind to dwell on the sense-objects — such a one, wholly deluded, is called a hypocrite.

Anyone who curbs the organs of action outwardly but dwells all the time on the objects of sense and gives free rein to his fancies, and then believes that he has attained to *naishkarmya* [freedom from the effects of action], such a person is sunk in ignorance and his claim is mere hypocrisy. A person who gets his hands tied up but in his mind strikes the enemy does in reality strike, though outwardly he does not seem to do so.

Please do not misunderstand what I have said. It does not mean that there is no scope for effort or striving, nor that, in that case, we had better act as we feel inclined to. We are constantly thinking of doing something or other, but reflection also helps us in restraining our hands. There can be no hypocrisy in ceaselessly fighting the enemy who holds us in his grip.

The point of the verse is that there should be no contradiction between thought and action. It is hypocrisy to yearn inwardly for an object and outwardly keep away from it. It is not hypocrisy if, despite one's best efforts, one does not succeed in always remaining vigilant, for the evil habit has had a long hold over us. Only, one should not merely try but also wish to remain vigilant. Hence, it is wrong for anyone who mentally dwells on objects of sense and outwardly shuns them to describe himself as a *sannyasi* or *yogi*.

The psychological effects of our actions in past lives cannot be wiped out all at once. Waves of desire will continue to rise. They will drench us again and again, but one day they will leave us dry.

(7) But he, O Arjuna, who, keeping all the senses under control of the mind, engages the organs in *karma yoga*, without attachment — that man excels."

(8) Do thou thy allotted task; for action is superior to inaction. With inaction even life's normal course is not possible.

(9) This world of men suffers bondage from all action save that which is done for the sake of sacrifice [*yajna*]. To this end, O Kaunteya, perform action without attachment.

We accept a broad definition of *yajna*. *Yajna* means any activity for the good of others. A man works for the good of others when he spends his body in their service. This should be done in a spirit of dedication to God. The word *yajna* comes from the root *yaj*, which means "to worship", and we please God by worshipping Him through physical labor. *Laborare est orare* — work is worship.

Among the Hindus, the practice of human sacrifice was prevalent at one time. Then followed animal sacrifice. Even today, thousands of goats are sacrificed to Mother Kali. The motive in this may be that of public good, but it is not a true sacrifice in which we kill other creatures. We serve the good of the world by refraining from causing suffering to them, because we shall refrain from doing so only if we cherish the lives of other creatures as we do our own.

We need not go into why in the past people performed — or even at the present time do perform — animal sacrifice. As man's beliefs become more enlightened, the meanings which people attach to certain words also become more enlightened. Even if Vyasa had defined the words which he used, we would ask why we should accept the meanings given by him. For instance, "noncooperation" has come to mean much more than we at first intended it to mean.

There is no harm in our enlarging the meaning of the word *yajna*, even if the new meaning we attach to the term was never in Vyasa's mind. We shall do no injustice to Vyasa by expanding the meaning of his words. Sons should enrich the legacy of their fathers. Why should we object if anyone regarded the spinning wheel with sentiments other than what we seek to create in the people about it? It is quite possible that in future people may see harm in the spinning wheel, may come to think that no one should wear cotton clothes at all, because they do harm. They may, for instance, believe that clothes should be made from fibres extracted from banana leaves.

If people should come to feel that way, anyone who still clings to the spinning wheel would be looked upon as a fool. A wise man, however, will mean by the spinning wheel not an article made of wood, but any type of work which provides employment to all people [cf. chapter two, verse 41]. That is also the case with regard to the meaning of the term *yajna*. Thus, we may — and should — attach to it a meaning not intended by Vyasa.

(10) Together with sacrifice did the Lord of beings create, of old, mankind, declaring, "By this shall ye increase. May this be to you the giver of all your desires."

"Along with *yajna* the Lord created men." Which type of *yajna* is meant here? Does the term have any special meaning? I think it has. The reference here is not to mental or intellectual work. Brahma did not ask human beings to multiply and prosper merely by working with their minds. What He meant was that they should do so through bodily *yajna*, by working with the body.

Scriptures of other religions enjoin the same thing. The Bible says, "With the sweat of thy brow thou shalt earn thy bread." Thus bodily labor is our lot in life. It is best, then, to do it in the spirit of service and dedicate it to Shri Krishna. Anyone who works in that spirit all his life becomes free from evil and is delivered from all bonds.

(11) "With this may you cherish the gods and may the gods cherish you. Thus cherishing one another may you attain the highest good."

So long as a person has someone in sight for whom he works, he is not engaged in service. Real service consists in working for those whom one does not know personally. The 330,000 gods belong to the world of imagination. We cannot see these gods, and yet we cultivate a living relationship with them. By and by, the sphere of our service will enlarge itself to embrace the whole world. We have thus left aside the word "gods" and interpreted the verse to mean that we should serve the humblest human beings, even those whom we never see, with respect and honor and looking upon them as gods and not as our servants. We should, in other words, serve the whole world.

This verse tells us that we should undertake bodily labor to do service. Man simply cannot live without such work. If he had not violated this law, he would not suffer as much as he does, the rich would not have become masters of immeasurable stores of wealth and the millions would not be suffering in poverty. God is a great economist. He is omnipotent. God never stores, for he can destroy and create the universe with a mere thought. He wants us, therefore, to provide only for each day. If we want anything the next day, we must labor for it.

(12) "Cherished with sacrifice, the gods will bestow on you the desired boons." He who enjoys their gifts without rendering aught unto them is verily a thief.

"Gods" in verses 11 and 12 must be taken to mean the whole creation of God. The service of all created beings is the service of the gods and the same is sacrifice.

(13) The righteous men who eat the residue of the sacrifice are freed from all sin; but the wicked who cook for themselves eat sin.

Those holy persons who eat only what is left behind after the *yajna* is over become free from all sins. They who first offer to society, to Shri Krishna, what they get to eat, live free from sin.

(14) From food springs all life, from rain is born food. From sacrifice comes rain and sacrifice is the result of action.

Can rain have any connection at all with whether we lead sinful or virtuous lives? It may have, but we do not know how. No event or action is without its effect.

(15) Know that action springs from *Brahman* [the supreme, impersonal God] and *Brahman* from the Imperishable; hence the all-pervading *Brahman* is ever firm-founded on sacrifice.

In every *yajna* God's presence may be felt, and where there is no *yajna* of body labor, God, too, is absent (though, of course, we believe that God is present everywhere). Human beings go on working with their bodies and that keeps the cycle going.

(16) He who does not follow the wheel thus set in motion here below, he, living in sin, sating his senses, lives, O Partha, in vain.

The earth rotates ceaselessly all the twenty-four hours of the day, and anyone who merely rests on it doing nothing lives to no purpose.

One who is always engaged in *yajna* is not subject to the binding effects of *karma*; but he who, disinclined to work, says, "I am *Brahman*," in justification of his idleness, is stated by the Gita to be living in sin. This is what Narasinha Mehta meant when he wrote that those who renounce the world will not win deliverance and those who enjoy life will. Here, "those who enjoy life" means all the people in the world who labor with their bodies and "those who renounce the world" means the incorrigible idlers.

(17) But the man who revels in *Atman*, who is content in *Atman*, for him no action exists.

(18) He has no interest whatever in anything done, nor in anything not done, nor has he need to rely on anything for personal ends.

(19) Therefore, do thou ever perform without attachment the work that thou must do; for performing action without attachment man attains the Supreme.

(20) For through action alone Janaka and others achieved perfection. Even with a view to the guidance of mankind thou must act.

(21) Whatever the best man does is also done by other men. What example he sets, the world follows.

People will adopt the standards which such a person sets. They will always observe what the eminent do. To what extent does Gandhi follow Truth in life?

Today is the birthday celebration of Rama [Ramanavami]. On this day we have a reading from the Ramayana for two hours and, in the morning, there is a discourse on the incarnation of Rama. People fast, or take only one meal, or eat only fruit. We shall put into practice what we have learnt from the Gita by celebrating the Ramanavami today in his manner.

I am faced with a conflict of duties. Though I am in the ashram, I may not be able to join in the celebration. There is another duty I have to discharge. Pandit Motilal has written to me and asked me to send for a certain person and discuss some matters with him. I shall, therefore, be in the ashram but engaged in discussions with him. When the Ramayana is being read, I shall be busy looking after the preparations for his lunch.

All this is wrong. If I had become totally absorbed with all these activities in the ashram and made it a rule to join in every celebration as I unfailingly attend prayers at four in the morning, I would have told Motilalji that today being Ramanavami I would be able to free myself only for half the day; but I do not yet have such firmness of mind, and, therefore, cannot act in that manner. It would not seem natural in me to do so.

I often feel that, as your leader, I should set an example in every matter; but I cannot do so unless there is complete harmony between my thought, speech and action. You should, of course, go on with the usual program. Keep a fast and have a reading from the Ramayana. Please bear with my deficiency, and see that you do not follow this weakness of mine after I am dead.

(22) For me, O Partha, there is naught to do in the three worlds, nothing worth gaining that I have not gained; yet I am ever in actition.

An objection is sometimes raised that God, being impersonal, is not likely to perform any physical activity. At best He may be supposed to act mentally. This is not correct; for the unceasing movement of the sun, the moon, the earth, etc. signifies God in action. This is not mental but physical activity.

Though God is without form and impersonal, He acts as though He had form and body. Hence though He is ever in action, He is free from action, unaffected by action. What must be borne in mind is that, just as all nature's movements and processes are mechanical and yet guided by divine intelligence or will, even so man must reduce his daily conduct to mechanical regularity and precision, but he must do so intelligently. Man's merit lies in observing divine guidance at the back of these processes and in an intelligent imitation of it, rather than in emphasizing the mechanical nature thereof and reducing himself to an automaton.

One has but to withdraw the self, withdraw attachment to fruit from all action, and then not only mechanical precision but security from all wear and tear will be ensured. Acting thus man remains fresh until the end of his days. His body will perish in due course, but his soul will remain evergreen without a crease or wrinkle.

(23) Indeed, for were I not, unslumbering, ever to remain in action, O Partha, men would follow my example in every way.

(24) If I were not to perform my task, these worlds would be ruined. I should be the cause of chaos and of the end of all mankind.

(25) Just as, with attachment, the unenlightened perform all actions, O Bharata, even so, but unattached, should the enlightened man act, with a desire for the welfare of humanity.

(26) The enlightened may not confuse the mind of the unenlightened, who are attached to action; rather must he perform all actions unattached, and thus encourage them to do likewise.

A wise man should not confuse the judgment of ignorant people who are attached to the work which they do; should not, for instance, ask them to go without a thing because he can do so. Shri Krishna said a little earlier that if he did not work for the people, there would be confusion of classes in society. He says the same thing in this verse in different words. If Arjuna took any unexpected step, people would not understand his intention and might do something which he had never wanted them to do. He had asked those hundreds of thousands of men to assemble there ready for battle. How could he, now, cause confusion in their minds? He should, therefore, go on doing his duty in the spirit of *yoga*, unattached to the fruits of his work, and inspire others to work likewise.

(27) All action is entirely done by the *gunas* of *prakriti*. Man, deluded by the sense "I", thinks, "I am the doer";

(28) But he, O Mahabahu, who understands the truth of the various *gunas* and their various activities knows that it is the *gunas* that operate on the *gunas*. He does not claim to be the doer.

This verse presents a problem, for its meaning has been completely perverted. It is interpreted without any reference to the context. There was a libertine in Rajkot. He used this verse to justify his dissolute life. He was a student of the *shastras* and could cite appropriate Sanskrit verses, on occasion, and so enjoyed a good status in society. He used to say that nature followed its own urges and that, therefore, he was not to blame, that he was untouched by either sin or virtue; but the man who is full of ignorant attachment and thinks little cannot take cover behind this verse.

The point of this verse is, in the extremely difficult business of running this world, in the running of this intricate machine (the very thought of which is sufficient to make one's head spin), what is there that I can do? What strength have I? I dare not touch a single part of it. Anyone who considers carefully how this world is kept going will see that the different *gunas* are ceaselessly active and doing their work.

Let us take the small example of the spinning-wheel. Suppose for a moment that the spindle became conceited. Its part in the working of the wheel is quite small. It has no motion of its own, and if it believed itself or the string to be the source of the motion, it would commit a grievous error. If it decides to become bent, it would produce a discordant note while rotating. It might feel that, instead of rotating monotonously, it was now moving in a novel manner, but it would soon lose its place. When dying, it might perhaps realize that it had made a terrible mistake, that its pride had cost it its very life.

Let us suppose now that the spindle has no such pride. It will then think that its motion was not its own, that it contributed nothing to the spinning, the string did its work and the wheel did its. It might then say that the *gunas* operate on the *gunas* and that it was of no interest to itself how they worked. I must work, the spindle would tell itself, as a mere slave, otherwise I and my relations would be ruined. It would then feel no pride and would no longer be carried away by foolish notions. We could say of such a spindle that it had learnt wisdom.

The same argument applies to human beings. No one can go on indulging himself and then argue that his conduct was the result of the *gunas* doing their work according to their nature.

(29) Deluded by the *gunas* of *prakriti* men become attached to the activities of the *gunas*. He who knows the truth of things should not unhinge the slow-witted who have not the knowledge.

(30) Cast all thy acts on Me. With thy mind fixed on the indwelling *Atman*, and without any thought of fruit or sense of "mine", shake off thy fever and fight!

After explaining all this — after explaining what *karma* is and why one should act — Shri Krishna tells Arjuna that, dedicating every action to Him, having purified his mind, fixed it on his *Atman* and emptied it of all desires, and without entertaining any thought of gain, he should go on doing *karma* as a matter of duty and irrespective of whether or not he was likely to benefit. "You should," Shri Krishna says, "shed your attachment to the ego and work." That is, work with the thought that you are not the doer of the *karma* and its fruit is not meant for you to enjoy, acting as if you were a piece of inert matter like the spindle of the spinning wheel.

Shri Krishna asks Arjuna to banish all impatience and anxiety and then fight. When he says "fight", he means that Arjuna should do what he regards as his duty. If we could know every time what we should do, if everyone's duty in a given situation was evident to him, all of us would have the same ideas of duty; but that is not so. On the contrary, we have to reflect to discover what our duty is. We have to apply numerous tests and then only can we see what our duty is. That is why Shri Krishna asks Arjuna to be passion-free and do his duty. One can do one's duty only if one banishes all impatience and anxiety in regard to it.

(31) Those who always act according to the rule I have here laid down, in faith and without cavilling — they, too, are released from the bondage of their actions.

To do one's duty means to fight and struggle. Since every *karma* involves a choice, there is necessarily a struggle. Even though caught in this way, between opposites, you will have transcended them if you dedicate every action to Krishna, do everything without attachment or aversion, have faith in God and present every *karma* as a gift to Him.

(32) But those who cavil at the rule and refuse to conform to it are fools, dead to all knowledge. Know that they are lost.

(33) Even a man of knowledge acts according to his nature. All creatures follow their nature. What then will constraint avail?

This verse has been taken to mean that a wicked person can never reform himself; but this verse is not intended to discourage a man from struggling against his nature. The aspiration to realize God is also part of human nature. One must, of course, struggle to improve oneself; but if he does not succeed, neither will constraint help him.

Constraint here [*nigraha*] means trying to control oneself or others. One may try to control a friend, or one's wife or sister or pupil, if they wish to reform themselves; but what can we do if they oppose us? What can even an emperor do to a person who has abandoned all shame? No one will succeed in his efforts to reform such a person.

We can offer *satyagraha* only against a person who has some love in his heart. We can control another only if there is mutual love between us. Where there is no such love, the only course for us is noncooperation with the other party.

(34) Each sense has its settled likes and dislikes towards its objects. Man should not come under the sway of these, for they are his besetters.

Hearing, for instance, is the object of the ears, which may be induced to hear something and disinclined to hear something else. Man may not allow himself to be swayed by these

likes and dislikes, but must decide for himself what is condu-
cive to his growth, his ultimate end being to reach the state
beyond happiness and misery.

(35) Better one's own duty, bereft of merit, than another's
well performed. Better is death in the discharge of one's
duty. Another's duty is fraught with danger.

One man's duty may be to serve the community by working as a sweeper, another's may be to work as an accountant. An
accountant's work may be more inviting; but that need not draw
the sweeper away from his work. Should he allow himself to be
drawn away he would himself be lost and put the community
into danger. Before God the work of man will be judged by the
spirit in which it is done, not by the nature of the work, which
makes no difference whatsoever. Whoever acts in a spirit of
dedication fits himself for salvation

It would not be right for Arjuna to think of retiring to a
forest and spending his days telling beads on the rosary. His
duty was to fight and kill. Retiring to a forest may be the right
course for a *rishi*, it was not so for Arjuna. Even if the *dharma*
meant for Arjuna seemed less worthy, for him it was the best.

Arjuna said:

(36) Then what impels man to sin, O Varshneya, even
against his will, as though by force compelled?

The Lord said:

(37) It is lust, it is wrath, born of the *guna, rajas*. It is the
arch-devourer, the arch-sinner. Know this to be man's enemy here.

One cause is *kama*, desire. It is man's evil thoughts which drive him to evil deeds. The second cause is anger. We get angry when we do not get the thing we want. Anger has its source in *rajas*. These two great energies of man drive him to sin. The reign of *kama* is different in its effect from the reign of Rama. Those who prosper under Rama's reign understand the sport of God which this creation is. Those, on the other hand, who are swayed by desire and anger will see, in the creation, not Rama's sport, but Satan's.

(38) As fire is obscured by smoke, a mirror by dirt, and the embryo by the amnion, so is knowledge obscured by this.

(39) Knowledge is obscured, O Kaunteya, by this eternal enemy of the wise man in the form of lust, the insatiable fire.

(40) The senses, the mind and the reason are said to be its seat. By means of these it obscures knowledge and stupefies man.

(41) Therefore, O Bharatarshabha, bridle thou first the senses and then rid thyself of this sinner, the destroyer of knowledge and discrimination.

(42) Subtle, they say, are the senses. Subtler than the senses is the mind. Subtler than the mind is the reason; but subtler even than the reason is He.

(43) Thus realizing Him to be subtler than the reason, and controlling the self by the Self (*Atman*), destroy, O Mahabahu, this enemy — lust, so hard to overcome.

When man realizes Him, his mind will be under His control, not swayed by the senses. And when the mind is conquered, what power has lust? It is indeed a subtle enemy, but when once the senses, the mind and the reason are under the control of the subtlemost Self, lust is extinguished.

"Controlling the self by the Self" means overcoming the baser, the demoniac impulses in the mind through the *Atman*, that is, through the godward impulses. In other words, Arjuna should, Shri Krishna tells him, master his egoistic instincts by striving for spiritual welfare.

Chapter Four

The Lord said:

(1) I expounded this imperishable *yoga* to Vivasvan. Vivasvan communicated it to Manu, and Manu to Ikshvaku.

(2) Thus handed down in succession, the royal sages learnt it. With long lapse of time it dwindled away in this world, O Parantapa.

We are doing things every moment, but it is God who has placed us on his wheel and is moving it like a potter, producing ever new shapes. "This *yoga* was known from the beginning of time, but has perished in this age. People have forgotten the art of working without attachment and aversion. Were it not so," Shri Krishna says, "I would not have had to be a witness to this battle."

(3) The same ancient *yoga* have I expounded to thee today, for thou art My devotee and My friend, and this is the supreme mystery.

The highest truth may be imparted only to a *bhakta* [devotee], for such a person will serve the world's good.

Arjuna said:

(4) Later was Thy birth, my Lord; earlier that of Vivasvan. How then am I to understand that Thou didst expound it in the beginning?

Chapter Four

The Lord said:

(5) Many births have we passed through, O Arjuna, both thou and I. I know them all, thou knowest them not, O Parantapa.

When we sing about the succession of births for human beings through 8,400,000 living forms, we refer to our having had countless lives before the present one, and we state our inference that death is only a change from an old house into a new one; but it is only a person who remembers his previous lives that can say this with certainty. Shri Krishna states categorically that, being a *yogi*, he remembers his previous existences but that Arjuna cannot remember his. He could say this; we cannot.

(6) Though unborn and inexhaustible in My essence, though Lord of all beings, yet assuming control over My nature, I come into being by My mysterious power.

The Hindu belief in *avatars* [incarnations of God] may present a difficulty to some of us. *Avatar* means descent. Our descent means God's descent too, for He is present in every creature and in every object. It would be correct to say, if we can say it without egotism, that each one of us is an *avatar*.

But, strictly speaking, it is not as if God comes down from above. When Krishna says that He incarnates Himself as a human being, he only uses the idiom of common speech. God never incarnates Himself as an *Atman* and is never born as a human being. He is ever the same. He is that through which we come into being and that through which we exist. When, from our human point of view, we see special excellence in some individual, we look upon him as an *avatar*.

(7) For whenever Right declines and Wrong prevails, then, O Bharata, I come to birth.

In these lines Shri Krishna held out an assurance to the entire world. If God remained inactive when *dharma* was eclipsed, man would be helpless. In this *Kaliyuga* [our present, fallen, age], all human efforts produce results contrary to what was intended. Hindus and Muslims, for instance, continue to fight among themselves. Can anyone prevent this? I was passionately eager to do such penance that they should never fight, but all my efforts failed. Does that mean that this fighting will go on forever? Assuredly not.

God tells us that He will tolerate our self-indulgence within limits, for He knows that we will weary of it. I will tolerate, He says, a little fighting and will not incarnate on the earth just because of that; but when men recognize no limits in fighting, demolish temples and kill people indiscriminately, that would mean eclipse of *dharma*. That would be wickedness in the name of *dharma*, it would mean the spread of *adharma* and disorder. "Do not," God says to comfort men, "give way to despair when such things happen. It is good," He says, "that you feel helpless at such a time, for by making you feel so I humble your pride."

We remember what Surdas says. "I have tried my strength in one way and another, till I am weary and can do no more. You must save me now." That is how man thinks in his pride— that he will do this, and he will do that; but God humbles his pride.

Man has this promise from the Lord: He need not despair and feel that, if he fails in some task, it will not be done. Let him have faith that God will have it done. So the Lord has said in these lines that, whenever necessary, He comes down to live on the earth, and sets everything right (see verse 8). If He did not do that, He would not enjoy our worship and reverence.

(8) To save the righteous, to destroy the wicked, and to reestablish Right I am born from age to age.

Here is comfort for the faithful and affirmation of the truth that Right ever prevails. Inscrutable Providence — the unique power of the Lord — is ever at work. This fact is *avatara*, incarnation.

The assurance which God holds out here is that when evil spreads in the world, some persons, inspired by God, feel in their hearts that it is not enough for them to be a little good, that they must be exceptionally good, so good that people would look upon them as a perfect manifestation of the Divine in man. That is how Shri Krishna came to be worshipped as the fullest *avatar*. God has in these verses assured man that whenever *dharma* is eclipsed and the reign of *adharma* spreads, He comes into the world to protect the good, to destroy the wicked and restore the rule of *dharma*. This means that *dharma* is never destroyed. Shri Krishna did not say that while the wicked are destroyed, the good are not. He himself passed away, and that too meeting an untimely death.

If we take a total view, we shall see that it is not wickedness but goodness which rules the world. The wicked can prevail only when they number multitudes, but goodness will rule when embodied to perfection even in one person. Nonviolence has been described as so powerful that all forces of violence subside in its presence. Under its influence, even beasts forget their nature. Even one good person can change the world. Such a one enjoys an empire over people's hearts. We do not, because we follow goodness only as best we may; but the type of good man

I have mentioned has but to send a message, and people will do what he wants them to do, such is the power of goodness.

Where wickedness prevails, there is disorder in every field of life, but where goodness rules, order prevails and people are happy. They are happy not in the sense that their material needs are satisfied, but in the sense that they lead virtuous and contented lives. As for material possessions, some men have fortunes in rupees and yet have a distracted life. That is no sign of being happy.

This verse, then, means that when *adharma* spreads, some men undertake *tapascharya* [the practice of austerities] and, through their *tapascharya*, generate goodness in the world. Even the wicked bow in reverence to their goodness. Its power is felt by beasts, too. This can happen even in the present age. Anyone who has completely shed hatred and ill will, who has succeeded in making his life a perfect embodiment of Truth, can command everything in life. He does not have to ask that anything be done. He has only to wish and the wish will be fulfilled.

(9) He who knows the secret of this My divine birth and action is not born again. After leaving the body, he comes to Me, O Arjuna.

For, when a man is secure in the faith that Right always prevails, he never swerves therefrom, pursuing to the bitterest end and against serious odds; and as no part of the effort proceeds from his ego, but all is dedicated to Him, being ever one with Him, he is released from birth and death.

(10) Freed from passion, fear and wrath, filled full with Me, relying on Me, and refined by the fiery ordeal of knowledge, many have become one with Me.

(11) In whatever way men resort to Me, even so do I render to them. In every way, O Partha, the path men follow is Mine.

Verse 11 has a history behind it. When Tilak [a leader of the Indian independence movement and an authority on the Gita] was alive, he cited this verse in the course of a discussion about violence and nonviolence. I argued that we should bear with a person who might have slapped us. In reply, he cited this verse to prove that the Gita upheld the principle of "tit for tat." That is, we should act towards a person as he acts towards us. I cling to the reply which I gave to him then. I argued that this verse could not be used in support of his contention. We should not act towards a person as he acts towards us. If he is bad to us, we may not therefore be bad to him. This verse merely lays down God's law. Shri Krishna says that He will worship a person as the latter worships Him. That means, we reap as we sow.

One cannot do evil to others and expect good for oneself. Man has no right to return two slaps for one. But a principle quite the opposite of this prevails in the world, and as education spreads the position becomes worse. Uncivilized people may return two slaps for one, may fight back when attacked, and among them the relation of father and son may not be always sweet. If, however, a father behaves as a civilized man, he would use wisdom and endure the son's misconduct in patience, and so teach him to behave with humility. If the son is good, then he would suffer his parents' weaknesses in patience, and that is the better way of the two.

Besides, we read in the preceding verse about the type of man who can realize God. It says that those serene persons who are who are free from all attachment, fear and anger, realize God. The present verse cannot contradict that one, but completes its meaning. The previous verse says that a person who yields to attachment and anger will not realize God. If one yields to anger, one will reap the fruit of anger. We are thus taught not to yield to anger but to banish attachment, fear and anger from us.

(12) Those who desire their actions to bear fruit worship the gods here; for in this world of men the fruit of actions is quickly obtainable.

Gods must not be taken to mean the heavenly beings of tradition, but whatever reflects the divine. In that sense man is also a god. Steam, electricity, and the other great forces of nature are all gods. Propitiation of these forces quickly bears fruit, as we well know, but it is short-lived. It fails to bring comfort to the soul and it certainly does not take one even a short step towards salvation.

(13) The order of the four *varnas* [castes] was created by Me according to the different *gunas* and *karma* of each. Yet know that, though author thereof, being changeless, I am not the author.

"I have," Shri Krishna says, "created four *varnas* on the basis of character and work." These are Brahmin, Kshatriya, Vaisya and Sudra. What should be the character of a Brahmin? What is distinctive of him? He is a Brahmin who knows *Brahman*, who lives most in the consciousness of God. And a Brahmin's work in life is to teach and help people to realize God. Besides this particular gift, he will also have the qualities of character which mark the other *varnas*. The Kshatriya's special *dharma* is protection of society. He should, above all, be a brave man. The Vaisya occupies himself with commerce. That is his special *dharma*. If he did not follow it, perhaps the world would not go on as it does. The Sudra's special *dharma* is service. If he combines with his service the spirit of *yajna*, or the motive of public good, he will win the reward of his life. There is here no question of higher and lower. If we regard the person who cleans lavatories as lower and another who reads the Gita as higher, that will be the end of us.

Anyone for whom action is a necessity is subject to continual change. God, being perfect, is under no necessity to act or do anything. He is present in everything that exists. Since the universe displays some order in its running we may assume that God is the author of that order; but the Lord has told us here that He is its author and yet is not its author — that is His mystery beyond human understanding.

(14) Actions do not affect Me, nor am I concerned with the fruits thereof.

God works like a machine. He is His law. He is the author of law and He it is who administers it. What perfect order this represents! There is never a question of His suspending His law or of deciding to uphold it. The machine has been going on from eternity. God's law exists and has been in operation since the time that He came into being, if we can say such a thing about Him.

If, in the same manner, we become totally immersed in our work so that we are one with our work, we lose ourselves in that work; but, then we should first ascertain our duty. Our duty is to strive for self-realization and we should lose ourselves in that aim. Such a person can never be disturbed by evil desire and, at last, becomes one with God. If we lose ourselves in God, become machines, make ourselves as clay in God's hands, is it any wonder that we may become one with Him?

(14, continued) Anyone who knows this truth about Me is never bound by *karma*.

How can he be? He who knows God's law will work but will desire nothing through work. Why do we feel the strain of work? Because, as we work, we remain attached to the "I" within us. Were it not so, we would never feel impatient or worried. We should be so absorbed in our work that we do not even notice the time when we should stop it. We should thus work on like machines. A person who works with such devotion, how can he suffer the effects of *karma*? That is, he never feels the strain of work. He is ever fresh.

(15) Knowing this did men of old, desirous of freedom, perform action. Do thou, then, just as they did — the men of old in days gone by.

The seekers of *moksha* in old days knew this truth and worked in such a spirit. To realize God means to work like God, with single-minded devotion and ceaseless vigilance. Though living in the human body, we should imitate God as much as we can. "Our forefathers did this. You too," Shri Krishna tells Arjuna, "should act in the same manner."

You, students, should study with the same devotion as the *brahmacharis* [religious students who have taken vows of self-control] of old days. They bore themselves in such a manner that, though mere boys, they seemed to be grown-up, mature men. I speak of more than forty years ago. I distinctly remember that, at our place, in the absence of the priest, his young son read the Bhagavata, and he read it very well indeed. So good was the education he had received at home. He must have been barely fifteen. Those whom we describe as *brahmacharis* today must behave as the *brahmacharis* of old did. You should sit upright, like a pole. Practise prayers for a whole month, and then you will discover that you are making some progress.

(16) What is action? What inaction? — here even the wise are perplexed. I will then expound to thee that action knowing which thou shalt be saved from evil.

"I will explain to you what right *karma* is and, having understood it, you will save yourself from evil, from the round of birth and death."

Our eyes are closed with bandages, like those over the eyes of the bullock in the oil-press. These bandages are not eternal, but we let them stay because we have grown used to them as natural, as fear is natural to us. There was a lion cub who, having always lived among goats, would tremble with fear like a goat. Then a real lion happened to meet him, and he held a mirror before him. The cub roared and escaped from the company of the goats. This cub had not been forced to put a bandage over its eyes, the bandage had just grown of itself.

In the same way, everyone of us has the bandage of ignorance grown over the eyes, and we do not know that it is not our *dharma* to live in evil, to submit to the round of birth and death. Our *dharma* is to rise ever higher until at last we can rise no more. We can have no rest till we have reached the goal. There will be eternal peace when we have reached it, that is, the peace of *moksha*. If you are on the top of the Himalayas, you are certain to fall from there, the top itself will crumble one day. It will crumble because it is ever changing. There is no changing in the state of *moksha* and no falling from there.

Moksha means destruction of the shackles of birth and death, getting out of that round. It means deliverance from evil. If we meet a worthy *guru*, and he loosens the bandage of ignorance over our eyes and holds before us the mirror of knowledge, we will know what we are, will know whether we deserve to go from birth to birth or are fit for something else. In truth we deserve better than to follow this round. We belong to a higher station. We shall become fit for that station when the darkness of ignorance has vanished.

(17) For it is meet to know the meaning of action, of forbidden action, as also of inaction. Impenetrable is the secret of action.

One should know what *karma* is, what *vikarma* — that is, forbidden karma — is, and what *akarma* — that is, ceasing from *karma* — is. The truth about *karma* is a deep mystery.

(18) Who sees inaction in action and action in inaction, he is enlightened among men. He is a *yogi*,. He has done all he need do.

The aim of verse 18 is to show that one who does *karma* may still not be doing anything. I have in a previous discourse mentioned my own example and told you that if I worked with attachment to my ego there were occasions when I would become mad; but things go on and leave me unaffected because I do everything merely as my duty. Even if every boy here were to leave me, I would not shed one tear. I would, on the contrary, dance with joy like Narasinha Mehta and sing "Happy am I that the net is no more."

If we work in such a disinterested spirit, we can follow the example of the Lord who said that, though He had created society with its four classes, He was not their creator. That is so because of the principle that one may do *karma* and still not have done it.

We are caught in the motion of the wheel of this world. Our duty is to work ceaselessly as a part of this machine. We should spend every minute of our waking life in doing work which has fallen to our lot, and do it as if we are impatient over it and yet not be so, be calm in fact.

The bullock that keeps the water-wheel in motion goes round and round, but no bucket falls from its place. If it were not a bucket but our heart in that place, it might fall off. The bucket, however, does not fall off, it remains in its place, calm. We should be filled with such calm.

On the other hand, if our heart is agitated, we may rest from work but shall not have ceased from action, we would still be working. The bonds tighten round such a person and there is but misery in store for him. If he believes that those who let themselves be entangled in the affairs of life weave bonds of *karma* round them and that he himself is free, he will be under a delusion, for every thought is a form of *karma*.

Last evening, I rebuked some of the boys. On that, one of them told me that there was harshness in my voice and asked me if it was not a sign of anger in me. I said that I was not God. I only strive for perfection, but I am not fit to be anyone's *guru*. I am full of desires, and so, when I am excited, my voice is naturally raised. If I had succeeded in banishing every desire from me, I would be able to do as much work as I am doing now, but my voice would ever be the same. I aspire to reach such a state.

It is true that sometimes my voice is raised and there is a little flash of anger in my eyes. This is the state Arjuna had in mind when he asked the Lord how a person is overcome with evil desire against his will. I am still swayed by desire and anger. I say this to illustrate the truth that we cease from *karma* in the measure that we do *karma* without any thought of its fruit. If I run away from a task in despair, if I get upset or raise my voice because someone does not listen to me, I weave the bonds of *karma* round me.

Having undertaken a duty, having agreed to look after some children entrusted to me, and sharing the responsibility of bringing them up, how can I now run away from the task? If I retire to the heights of the Himalayas and live there in peace, I would be indulging my body in idle comfort and weave round myself the bonds of *karma*. I must, therefore, remain in the midst of these responsibilities, and win *moksha* through them.

Everyone should apply this illustration to himself, forgetting all about me as an individual. I have mentioned my own example merely in order to explain that we are all imperfect. I say, not merely out of modesty or as a matter of form, but with detachment, that I am imperfect. This is not my modesty, but the simple truth. When I am completely free from the sway of desire and anger, you will always see me calm, more so than you see me today. I am striving to be free from these. I feel that one day I shall attain such a state of calm.

(19) He whose every undertaking is free from desire and selfish purpose, and he who has burnt all his actions in the fire of knowledge — such a one the wise call a *pandita*.

(20) He who has renounced attachment to the fruit of action, who is ever content and free from all dependence — he, though immersed in action, yet acts not.

(21) Expecting naught, holding his mind and body in check, putting away every possession, and going through action only in the body, he incurs no stain.

The purest act, if tainted by self binds; but when it is done in a spirit of dedication, it ceases to bind. When self has completely subsided, it is only the body that works. For instance, in the case of a man who is asleep, his body alone is working. A prisoner doing his prison task has surrendered his body to the prison authorities and only his body, therefore, works. Similarly, he who has voluntarily made himself God's prisoner does nothing himself. His body mechanically acts. The doer is God, not he. He has reduced himself to nothingness.

(22) Content with whatever chance may bring, rid of the pairs of opposites, free from ill will, even-minded in success and failure, he is not bound, though he acts.

He who is satisfied with what he gets in the ordinary course of things, who has risen above the pairs of opposites such as happiness and suffering, has no ill will in him, bears an equal mind towards success and failure, and is indifferent towards them or is not affected by them — such a person does not dance with joy on getting something which is welcome to him and does not start lamenting his lot when disagreeable things happen. He may do *karma* and still be not doing it — that is, will not be bound by the effects of his *karma*.

(23) Of the free soul who has shed all attachment, whose mind is firmly grounded in knowledge, who acts only for sacrifice, all *karma* is extinguished.

Every *karma* done in the spirit of *yajna* [sacrifice] leaves no effects behind it. Any action done without reference to one's own interest is a form of *yajna*. The next verse follows as a consequence from this, and also explains the manner of doing such *yajna*.

(24) The offering of sacrifice is *Brahman*. The oblation is *Brahman*. It is offered by *Brahman* in the fire that is *Brahman*. Thus he whose mind is fixed on acts dedicated to *Brahman* must needs pass on to *Brahman*.

That which is thrown into the *yajna* is *Brahman* and so is the oblation. If that oblation is thrown by *Brahman* into the fire which is also *Brahman*, it is bound to act as *Brahman*. Anyone who relates all his *karmas* to *Brahman* will merge into the latter. Shri Krishna now explains the different types of *yajna*.

(25) Some *yogis* perform sacrifice in the form of worship of the gods. Others offer sacrifice of sacrifice itself in the fire that is *Brahman*.

I have been told by Vinoba [Gandhi student and Sanskrit scholar, Vinoba Bhave] that there is support in the Vedas for the view that a person who has attained to knowledge of the Brahman need not worry about performing *yajna*. One who has made his life itself a long *yajna*, why should he undertake any other *yajna*? But to a person who has made his whole life a *yajna*, doing a *yajna* comes most naturally. Such a person is ever engaged in doing *yajna* with ceaseless vigilance. He identifies himself with all creatures in their suffering. The meaning here is not that he gives up doing *yajna*. Rather, it becomes his very nature to engage himself in *yajna*, just as it is natural for God to dwell in the heart of the basest of human beings.

(26) Some offer as sacrifice the sense of hearing and the other senses in the fires of restraint. Others sacrifice sound and the other objects of sense in the fires of the senses.

(27) Others again sacrifice all the activities of the senses and of the vital energy in the *yogic* fire of self-control kindled by knowledge.

That is to say, they lose themselves in the contemplation of the Supreme. They stop the functioning of all sense organs, stop even the movement of *prana*, that is, breathing, make themselves motionless and, entering into *samadhi*, become firmly established in the *Atman* and, lighting this *yoga* with the fire of knowledge, make a sacrificial offering of all the organs into it. If a person cannot control his mind by any other means, he may adopt this way.

Or one may get angry with oneself and stop the functioning of all one's organs. The man who tries to observe *brahmacharya* [self-control; celibacy] but fails in his efforts may become desperate and undertake an indefinite fast, resolving in his mind that he will not let any organ of the body function because, so long as even one of them is functioning, his mind revels in evil thoughts. He may, therefore, decide that it is best to stop all organs from functioning. This is lighting up the fire of the *yoga* of control of the *Atman*.

A man striving for success in *brahmacharya* suffers pain as a woman in labor does. If a person cannot bear obstruction to his efforts to cultivate self-control, we see that he gets upset. This is why I often say that such a person is like a milk cow and that we should bear his kicks.

(28) Some sacrifice with material gifts, with austerities, with *yoga*, some with the acquiring and some with the imparting of knowledge. All these are sacrifices of stern vows and serious endeavour.

There are people in this world who perform the *yajna* of money — who let their wealth be shared by others. Some others perform *tapas* [austerities] and imprison the monkey which is our mind. Some others, still, practice *yoga* or devote themselves regularly to holy studies, to the study of the Vedas. Some perform the *yajna* of the pursuit of knowledge. They do not read, but devote themselves to reflection and meditation. Ascetics who put themselves under strict vows perform a *yajna* in that manner.

(29) Others absorbed in the practices of the control of the vital energy sacrifice the outward in the inward and the inward in the outward, or check the flow of both the inward and the outward vital airs.

Some throw *pranavayu* [breath in the lung] as sacrifice into *apanavayu* [breath in the abdomen], while others hold the latter in the former. Some others still hold both. All these are practitioners of *pranayama*.

(30) Yet others, abstemious in food, sacrifice one form of vital energy in another. All these know what sacrifice is and purge themselves of all impurities by sacrifice.

(31) Those who partake of the residue of sacrifice — called *amrita* (ambrosia) — attain to everlasting *Brahman*. Even this world is not for a non-sacrificer. How then the next, O Kurusattama?

To strive and conquer desire is also a form of *yajna*. The Gita teaches us to look upon all activities for the Supreme Good as forms of *yajna*. The idea that we work for others is only an illusion. We always work for ourselves. We shall attain deliverance only if we work exclusively for our higher Self. All activities for the Supreme Good, therefore, aim at one's own good.

Coming back to the verse, those who consume what remains after the *yajna* is over, that is, those who utilize for themselves only the time which remains after they have completed the *yajna*, enjoy *amrita* and attain to the timeless *Brahman*. The person who has done no work during the day but, like a heifer idling in mud, has spent his time in bed, steals the sleep which he enjoys at night. The man who does no *yajna* can win nothing in this world. What then can he win in the other world? He is lost in both.

Verse 31 has a wide meaning. It means that we should eat only after all others have had their food. So long as the embodied soul lives in this world, it has no choice but to have relations with others. To become disinterested in the body, therefore, means that one should devote oneself exclusively to the service of others so that one may attain the *Brahman* beyond time.

(32) Even so various sacrifices have been described in the Vedas. Know them all to proceed from action [*karma*]. Knowing this thou shalt be released.

Ordinarily the verse should mean this: "The Vedas describe these different types of *yajna*. You should know that all of them exist through *karma*. Only so can you win *moksha*." The Lord makes it clear in this verse that it is simply impossible for anyone to live without doing *karma*. That, of course, does not mean that a state of *akarma* is impossible. Every karma done for the good of the *Atman*, though it appears to be *karma*, is in reality *akarma*. If we can renounce the fruits of *karma* — that is work only for others — then we may work like horses. On the other hand, when working for ourselves, we should be like a piece of inert matter, have no interest in the work at all. This is a state of the heart, an attitude of mind. Anyone who cultivates that attitude towards everything he does — sleeping, eating, drinking or cleaning the lavatory — will attain to *moksha*.

(33) Knowledge-sacrifice is better, O Parantapa, than material sacrifice, for all action which does not bind finds its consummation in knowledge (*jnana*).

The person who performs the *yajna* of knowledge makes a greater sacrifice than another who performs the *yajna* of money, for the *yajna* of knowledge includes everything — money and all other things. Who does not know that works of charity performed without knowledge often result in great harm? Unless every act, however noble its motive, is informed with knowledge, it lacks perfection. Hence the complete fulfillment of all action is in knowledge.

(34) The masters of knowledge who have seen the Truth will impart to thee this knowledge. Learn it through humble homage and service and by repeated questioning.

"You can obtain this knowledge," Shri Krishna tells Arjuna, "by bowing before a *guru* in utmost humility, by prostrating yourself before him, by serving him and by frequent questioning — by harassing him with questions, and in no other way. The enlightened ones who have seen the truth will impart this knowledge to you."

(35) When thou hast gained this knowledge, O Pandava, thou shalt not again fall into such error. By virtue of it thou shalt see all beings without exception in thyself and thus in Me.

Once we have realized that this whole universe exists in God, how can there be any problem of violence and nonviolence for us? We would feel even thieves and tigers to be ourselves. Till we feel in that way, we may be sure that we have not attained to a state of knowledge at all.

Can we claim that we have the knowledge described in the verse which we have been discussing? Suppose that we learn in one day to recite it; do we then become seers of truth? Do we become so when we teach that verse to others? Of course not. We cannot have this knowledge merely by talking about it. We understand with our reason that the universe is the same as our-selves, but we can only imagine what that means. We cannot grasp the idea or feel its truth. The moment we leave this place, we shall treat all others as different from us. Only that person in whom this idea has sunk from the intellect to the heart — even an intellectual nincompoop can have a heart which is an ocean of compassion — can feel its truth in direct experience.

Shri Krishna says to Arjuna, "When I say that men of knowledge will impart this knowledge to you, I do not mean that they will convince your reason. I mean that they will awaken in you the faith that it is so. You will then realize that it is because of your reason that you see things as separate from one another, that in truth they are one." God, ourselves and all ob-jects in the universe are in essence one Reality. Even God van-ishes and we have only *"Neti, neti"* ["Not this, not this"; undiffer-entiated Truth]. When a person has realized this, his ignorance will have completely vanished.

(36) Even though thou be the most sinful of sinners, thou shalt cross the ocean of sin by the boat of knowl-edge.

For me, the Gita is the ship, not because it is a learned work but because I have liked it, it has appealed to me in my old age, and verses in it have been a great support to me.

(37) As a blazing fire turns its fuel to ashes, O Arjuna, even so the fire of knowledge turns all actions to ashes.

First, knowledge was compared to a ship, and now it is compared to fire. It burns up the bonds of *karma*.

Man does not live by bread alone. Whereas the lower creatures need only food to live, man lives by performing *yajna* [sacrifice]. Everyone performs *yajna* in one way or another. The spinning wheel is one type of *yajna*. Prayers, too, are a *yajna* for us. They represent a mode of spiritual cleansing. Till we have performed that *yajna*, we should feel uneasy inside us. Only those who attend to these readings of the Gita in that spirit, not others, may be said to be really interested in it.

We join these prayers in order that they may sustain us in our life. Man's need for prayer is as great as his need for bread. A bad man will use his ears to hear evil of others and see sinful things, but the good man says that, had he a thousand eyes and ears, he would use them to contemplate the vision of God for ever and to hear devotional songs, and employ his five thousand tongues to sing His praises. It is only after I have prayed here everyday that I feel the bliss of having tasted the *amrita* of knowledge. For that man who wishes to be a real human being, dal and roti are not his food. They count little to him. His real food is prayer.

You are *brahmacharis*. You ought to get up in time and attend prayers everyday. You may excuse yourselves from other duties, but never from prayers. You should cultivate such a state of mind that for half an hour you will have only one thought in your mind, and no other. Everyone should set apart some time in this manner for reflection. It provides an opportunity to feel one with all living creatures.

(38) There is nothing in this world so purifying as knowledge. He who is perfected by *yoga* finds it in himself in the fullness of time.

We see nothing in this world as holy as this knowledge. He who has become fit for *moksha* through the practice of *yoga* [discipline] comes to this knowledge in the course of time by his own effort. That knowledge is realization of the self. As soon as this realization is attained, all the burden of this body and of *karma* will melt away.

(39) It is the man of faith who gains knowledge — the man who is intent on it and who has mastery over his senses. Having gained knowledge, he comes ere long to the supreme peace.

We do a sum in mathematics with the help of our reasoning faculty. It does not matter whether or not we have faith in mathematics; but for spiritual knowledge, faith is essential. Does a child have to train his intellect in order to love its mother or father? An illiterate mother loves her child with her heart.

That person who is for ever devoted to the Lord, who is self-controlled, who has perfect control over every sense, attains this knowledge and soon wins peace — *moksha* — through it.

(40) But the man of doubt, without knowledge and without faith, is lost. For him who is given to doubt there is neither this world nor that beyond, nor happiness.

That person who does not value knowledge, who lacks faith, that is, who is a skeptic, will perish. He prospers neither in this world nor in the other.

(41) He who has renounced all action by means of *yoga*, who has severed all doubt by means of knowledge — him, self-possessed, no actions bind, O Dhananjaya.

(42) Therefore, with the sword of self-realization sever thou this doubt, bred of ignorance, which has crept into thy heart. Betake thyself to *yoga* and arise, O Bharata!

"Therefore," Shri Krishna says, "the doubt in your heart, born of ignorance, destroy it with the sword of knowledge and take up *yoga* — *karma yoga* — and get ready."

Chapter Five

Arjuna said:

(I) Thou laudest renunciation of actions, O Krishna, whilst at the same time thou laudest performance of action. Tell me for a certainty which is the better.

A person may be eating with proper attention and yet we may say of him that he is, nevertheless, not eating. Of whom can we say this? Of one who eats as though he was performing a *yajna*, who offers up his action of eating to Shri Krishna, who eats with the feeling that he does so in obedience to the Lord's command.

Or, such a person may tell himself that it is not he, but his body, that is eating — the *Atman* does not eat, or drink or sleep. He will then eat to serve others, to serve the lame, the crippled and the afflicted. That will be service of God, for God who dwells in the afflicted is also like them. That person's *karma* of eating will be in truth *akarma*, and will not bind him.

If we aspire to be good, we must ceaselessly work to serve others, serve them in a perfectly disinterested spirit. We should not serve anyone with the hope that he, too, will serve us one day, but we may serve him because the Lord dwells in him and we serve that Lord. If we hear anyone crying in distress for help, we should immediately run to him and help him. We should help the Lord crying in distress. After doing what was needed, we should feel that it was all a dream.

The Lord said:

(2) Renunciation and performance of action both lead to salvation; but of the two, *karma yoga* (performance) is better than *sannyasa* (renunciation).

Man cannot completely refrain from *karma*, and therefore, it is easy for everyone to follow *karma yoga*. Renunciation of *karma*, on the other hand, is a difficult matter, for it requires knowledge, whereas *karma yoga* can be followed even by an ordinary person. To retire into a cave in the Himalayas and sit there forever doing nothing — it is extremely difficult to succeed in such an effort. It is a hard task to cultivate such stillness that one would not be tempted by anything even in one's thoughts. The Lord, therefore, tells us that *karma yoga* is a better path, since the other one is beset with obstacles and is likely to encourage hypocrisy, while the *karma yogi* runs no such risk.

(3) Him one should know as ever renouncing who has no dislikes and likes; for he who is free from the pairs of opposites is easily released from bondage.

(4) It is the ignorant who speak of *Sankhya* and *yoga* as different, not so those who have knowledge. He who is rightly established even in one wins to the fruit of both.

Sankhya here means renunciation and *yoga* means *karma yoga*. Men of little understanding think them to be distinct from each other, but not so the wise. In truth, they are two sides of the same coin. Anyone who becomes established in either reaps the fruit of success in the other, too.

A thing at rest and another in intense motion seem alike;

the earth, for instance. Rest and motion are a pair of opposites; but he who remains unaffected by such opposites reaps the fruit of both.

(5) The goal that the *Sankhyas* attain is also reached by the *yogis*. He sees truly who sees both *Sankhya* and *yoga* as one.

(6) But renunciation, O Mahabahu, is hard to attain except by *yoga*. The ascetic equipped with *yoga* attains *Brahman* ere long.

For him who has not learnt to offer all his actions to Shri Krishna, *sannyasa* is extremely difficult to practice. The truth is that *sannyasa* is impossible to practice except through *karma yoga*. Really speaking, therefore, *sannyasa* is *karma yoga*, and nothing else. He who has become free from attachments and aversions, who has shed the "I" in him, has become a true *sannyasi*.

(7) The *yogi* who has cleansed himself, has gained mastery over his mind and all his senses, who has become one with the *Atman* in all creation, although he acts he remains unaffected.

(8) The *yogi* who has seen the Truth knows that it is not he that acts — whilst seeing, hearing, touching, smelling, eating, walking, sleeping or breathing,

(9) Talking, letting go, holding fast, opening or closing the eyes — in the conviction that it is the senses that are moving in their respective spheres.

Verses 8 and 9 are a commentary on the preceding verse. The man who knows the Truth acts as if he himself did nothing. Whether seeing or hearing, smelling, eating, walking, lying down to sleep, breathing, speaking, parting with or accepting anything, winking — in all these he will feel that it is his senses which are functioning according to their nature. Such a person acts but does not do anything. Even when he retires to sleep, he will say that it is his body which will fall into sleep. We can thus take it as a mathematical truth that our work will tend to evil in proportion as we are conscious of the "I" in us, and it will tend to good in proportion as we shed that "I".

Only that person can apply these verses to himself who is always completely absorbed in the task at hand, whose every action is dedicated to Shri Krishna and who seeks no benefit for himself from anything he does. If he uses his ears, it is to hear praise of God. If he uses his eyes, it is to see the Lord. Nor does he ever suffer. Whenever anything happens which might cause him pain, he would think that the pain was not felt by him. "If," he would tell himself, "I forget the 'I' in me when suffering this pain and think of Rama, no one would be able to know that I had been stung by a scorpion." He would feel that it had stung his body and that there was a red spot on it, that is all. He works mechanically, and still everything he does shines out. His actions grow ever more beautiful. He never tires of work, never feels upset and confused.

(10) He who dedicates his actions to *Brahman* and performs them without attachment is not smeared by sin, as the lotus leaf by water.

The term "sin" is used here in a wide sense, and covers both sin and virtue. Such a person does not have to suffer the consequences of either sinful or virtuous action. He goes on working, but remains unaffected by work. Leaves of other plants get wet and decay, but the lotus is not moistened by water.

(11) Only with the body, mind and intellect, and also with the senses, do the *yogis* perform action without attachment for the sake of self-purification.

(12) A man of *yoga* obtains everlasting peace by abandoning the fruit of action. The man ignorant of *yoga*, selfishly attached to fruit, remains bound.

Renouncing the fruits of *karma*, the *yogi* wins the peace which is the reward of faith and devotion, the peace which brings *moksha*, the peace enjoyed by the man established in *Brahman*. That is not the peace of a stone or the peace which the unthinking man enjoys, or that which the man of lust absorbed in the pursuit of lust enjoys for a while. It is the peace of the man established in *Brahman*, the bliss which belongs to the *Atman*.

The man who is not established in *yoga* stays in the grip of desire. He who works under the sway of ignorance must be a man attached, that is, one who is bound through attachment to the fruits of work, or by the snakelike coil of expectation and sense-cravings.

(13) Renouncing with the mind all actions, the dweller in the body who is master of himself rests happily in his city of nine gates, neither doing nor getting anything done.

To renounce all *karma* mentally means to make the mind indifferent to them, to withdraw it into an attitude of detachment towards work and feel that we are not doing what we are engaged in, that it is God who impels us to do it. Surely we do not feel, as we breathe, that we are breathing. We have mentally renounced that *karma*. It becomes necessary to breathe with a conscious effort of mind only when natural breathing is obstructed. At all other times, it goes on mechanically.

The *Atman* dwells, ever at rest, in this body with nine doors [eyes, ears, nostrils, mouth and the two organs of excretion] doing nothing and causing nothing to be done. Though it may be working or acting to make others work, it will not be doing so if it has mentally renounced *karma*.

(14) The Lord creates neither agency nor action for the world; neither does He connect action with its fruit. It is nature that is at work.

God is no doer. The inexorable law of *karma* prevails, and in the very fulfillment of the law — giving everyone his deserts, making everyone reap what he sows — lies God's abounding mercy and justice.

In undiluted justice is mercy. Mercy which is inconsistent with justice is not mercy but its opposite; but man is not a judge knowing past, present, and future. So for him mercy or forgiveness is the purest justice. Being himself ever liable to be judged, he must accord to others what he would accord to himself, viz. forgiveness. Only by cultivating the spirit of forgiveness can he reach the state of a *yogi*, whom no actions bind, the man of even-mindedness, the man skilled in action.

(15) The Lord does not take upon Himself anyone's vice or virtue. It is ignorance that veils knowledge and deludes all creatures.

---

(16) But to them whose ignorance is destroyed by the knowledge of *Atman*, this knowledge, like the sun, reveals the Supreme.

When a man's ignorance, which envelops the knowledge in him, has been destroyed by that knowledge, this light of God is revealed to him.

God is the witness of all that occurs. The idea that we should live in obedience to Him, act only as prompted by Him — that is knowledge. We can experience its truth directly only when all the twists in the heart have straightened out and the *Atman* alone shines there forever.

(17) Those whose intellect is suffused with That, whose self has become one with That, who abide in That, and whose end and aim is That, wipe out their sins with knowledge, and go whence there is no return.

When the night in one's mind has turned to dawn, one comes in the presence of God.

(18) The men of self-realization look with an equal eye on a Brahmin possessed of learning and humility, a cow, an elephant, a dog and even a dog-eater.

Men of knowledge, see all things with an equal eye. They feel that the *Atman* in each of these is identical with the *Atman* in themselves. The only difference is that in some the *Atman* is enveloped by layers upon layers of ignorance, and in others these layers have fallen off. What was said earlier, that the *yogi* sees himself in others, means the same thing as this. Water of the Ganges in separate vessels is Ganges water after all.

(19) In this very body they have conquered the round of birth and death, whose mind is anchored in sameness; for perfect *Brahman* is same to all, therefore in *Brahman* they rest.

As a man thinks, so he becomes, and therefore those whose minds are bent on being the same to all achieve that sameness and become one with *Brahman*.

Let us describe an instance of equal regard for all. If an enemy and a friend arrive at his place together, both hungry, the self-realized man will offer food first to the enemy. He would feel that to be justice. He would be afraid lest there be some hatred for the enemy lurking in his heart, and he would satisfy him first. The friend, too, would appreciate his motive. If anyone warns him that feeding an enemy would be like giving milk to a snake, he would cite in reply this verse from the Gita.

One rule of *swadeshi* [the principle that one serve one's neighbor first] is that in serving people we should give priority to those who live near us. The reason behind this is that we cannot reach all human beings in this world. If you ignore your neighbor and seek to serve someone living far away, that would be pride on your part.

There is also an opposite rule — that we should serve first those who are distant from us and then those who are near us. Distant in this rule means distant from us mentally. We display good manners, culture and learning in serving first those who are mentally distant from us.

(20) He whose understanding is secure, who is undeluded, who knows *Brahman* and who rests in *Brahman*, will neither be glad to get what is pleasant, nor sad to get what is unpleasant.

(21) He who has detached himself from contacts without finds bliss in *Atman*. Having achieved union with *Brahman* he enjoys eternal bliss;

(22) For the joys derived from sense-contacts are nothing but mines of misery. They have beginning and end, O Kaunteya. The wise man does not revel therein.

(23) The man who is able, even here on earth ere he is released from the body, to hold out against the flood-tide of lust and wrath — he is a *yogi*. He is happy.

(24) He who finds happiness only within, rest only within, light only within — that *yogi*, having become one with nature, attains to oneness with *Brahman*.

(25) They win oneness with *Brahman* — the seers whose sins are wiped out, whose doubts are resolved, who have mastered themselves, and who are engrossed in the welfare of all beings.

Rishis who are sinless and pure attain to *Brahmanirvana*. *Rishis* of what description? Those whose doubts have vanished, who hold their *Atman* a prisoner (have control over it) and who rejoice in the good of all creatures.

Such a person can bear ill will to no one. He is ever ready to serve the welfare of even the most wicked. He serves the whole world.

(26) Rid of lust and wrath, masters of themselves, the ascetics who have realized *Atman* find oneness with *Brahman* everywhere around them.

(27) That ascetic is ever free who, having shut out the outward sense contacts, sits with his gaze fixed between the brows, outward and inward breathing in the nostrils made equal; his senses, mind, and reason, held in check; rid of longing, fear and wrath; and intent on Freedom.

These verses refer to some of the *yogic* practices laid down in the *yoga sutras*. A word of caution is necessary regarding these practices.

They serve for the *yogi* the same purpose as athletics and gymnastics do for one who pursues worldly pleasures. His physical exercises help the latter to keep his senses of enjoyment in full vigor. The *yogic* practices help the *yogi* to keep his body in condition and his senses in subjection. Men versed in these practices are rare in these days, and few of these turn them to good account.

He who has achieved the preliminary stage on the path of self-discipline, he who has a passion for freedom, and who, having rid himself of the pairs of opposites, has conquered fear, would do well to go in for these practices which will surely help him. It is such a disciplined man alone who can, through these practices, render his body a holy temple of God. Purity both of the mind and body is a *sine qua non*, without which these processes are likely, in the first instance, to lead a man astray and then drive him deeper into the slough of delusion.

That this has been the result in some cases many know from actual experience. That is why the prince of *yogis*, Patanjali gave the first place to *yamas* [cardinal vows] and *niyamas* [casual vows], and held as eligible for *yogic* practices only those who have gone though the preliminary discipline. The five cardinal vows are nonviolence, truth, non-stealing, celibacy and non-possession. The five casual vows are bodily purity, contentment, the study of the scriptures, austerity and meditation of God.

(29) Knowing Me as the acceptor of sacrifice and austerity, the great Lord of all the worlds, the friend of all creation, the *yogi* attains to peace.

This verse may appear to be in conflict with verses 14 and 15 of this chapter and similar ones in other chapters. It is not really so. Almighty God is Doer and non-Doer, Enjoyer and non-Enjoyer both. He is indescribable, beyond the upper power of human speech. Man somehow strives to have a glimpse of Him and in so doing invests him with diverse and even contradictory attributes.

Chapter Six

The last chapter raised the question, "Of *sannyasa* and *karma yoga*, which is superior?" Shri Krishna has tried to answer the question, but the problem is not one which can be easily solved. The personal God and the impersonal *Brahman* — both are real; and, likewise, he who rests in absolute peace and he who is ceaselessly occupied in work — both are right, for the *sannyasi* is in fact working and the other one who is always working rests in absolute peace.

But Arjuna does not say yet that he has understood the point, and so Shri Krishna takes up the same argument again in chapter six.

The Lord said:

(1) He who performs all obligatory action, without depending on the fruit thereof, is a *sannyasi* and a *yogi* — not the man who neglects the sacrificial fire nor he who neglects action.

He who deposits all his works in God's treasury and goes on doing his duty without looking for reward is both a *sannyasi* and a *yogi*; but that person who never lights the fire for sacrifice — originally it was an act of public service to keep a fire burning in the home for performing a sacrifice — or never works, is neither a *sannyasi* nor a *yogi*. Such a person would in fact be a prince of idlers.

(2) What is called *sannyasa*, know thou to be *yoga*, O Pandava; for none can become a *yogi* who has not renounced selfish purposes.

Sannyasa is not something which can be demonstrated outwardly; it is a matter of the spirit within. The restless play of desires and fancies should cease. Only then can one be a *sannyasi*.

(3) For the man who seeks to scale the heights of *yoga*, action is said to be the means. For the same man, when he has scaled those heights, repose is said to be the means.

For one who aspires to master *yoga*, the only means is work. If a person lets himself be beaten for a long time on the anvil of work, some day he may be shaped into a *yogi*. For him who has established himself in *yoga*, who has attained to a state of spiritual equipoise, whose mind has become steadfast, for such a person the right means (of continuing in this state) is *shama*, that is, resting in peace. Such peace is not the peace of the grave or the peace of lethargy or inertness. It is the peace of conscious life, the peace of the sea.

(4) When a man is not attached either to the objects of sense or to actions and sheds all selfish purpose, then he is said to have scaled the heights of *yoga*.

(5) By one's Self (*Atman*) should one raise oneself, and not allow oneself to fall; for *Atman* alone is the friend of self and *Atman* alone is self's foe.

The *Atman* has all the attributes of God, and that is why it can merge in Him. As the *Atman* is self-effulgent, so is God. A thing cannot merge in something else with unlike attributes.

(6) His Self alone is friend to one who has conquered himself by his Self; but to him who has not conquered himself and is thus inimical to himself, even his Self behaves as foe.

While we live, there are two sides in us: the demoniac and the divine, the godlike and the satanic. So long as this strife goes on, it is our duty to fight Satan and protect ourselves. In the war between gods and demons, it is the former who always win in the end. When the world is no more, God will laugh and ask where Satan was.

(7) Of him who has conquered himself and who rests in perfect calm, the Self is completely composed, in cold and heat, in pleasure and pain, in honor and dishonor.

Any praise or censure given to us is like a stream which flows away towards God and disappears.

(8) The *yogi* who is filled with the contentment of wisdom and discriminative knowledge, who is firm as a rock, who has mastered his senses, and to whom a clod of earth, a stone and gold are the same, is possessed of *yoga*.

Wisdom (*jnana*) here means listening to readings from the *shastras*, meditating over them, studying them, and discriminative knowledge (*vijnana*) means realizing the *Atman* in direct experience. *Jnana* is understanding through reason, and *vijnana* is that knowledge which sinks through reason into experience.

Nonviolence will have become direct experience for us in this sense when our whole life comes to be permeated with the spirit of compassion, when nonviolence manifests itself in us in its true essence. That boy who comes to feel compassion as his own experience will, to that extent, have purified himself, or attained knowledge of the Self.

He whose *Atman* is filled to perfect contentment with such *jnana* and *vijnana*, who has subdued his senses completely — such a one may be described as a *yogi* who has attained freedom. He has become united with God, has become inwardly purified.

To such a *yogi*, clay, stone and gold — all are equal. All three come from earth. Gold, silver, diamonds, sapphire — all these are transformations of earth; but they are all without any worth. Every one of them is but dust. If we shed greed, we would look upon all these articles with the same eye.

(9) He excels who regards alike the boon companion, the friend, the enemy, the stranger, the mediator, the alien and the ally, as also the saint and the sinner.

The same law applies to the world of the living which applies to the world of inert matter. As clay and gold are ultimately the same substance, so the *sadhu* (saint) and the sinner are ultimately one. They are both manifestations of the *Atman*. The layer of uncleanliness has disappeared from over the *sadhu's Atman* and is becoming ever thicker over the sinner's. We shall have risen above this ordinary level only when we learn to have equal regard for either.

(10) Let the *yogi* constantly apply his thought to *Atman*, remaining alone in a secluded place, his mind and body under control, rid of desires and possessions.

A *yogi* should constantly live in solitude and be in union with the *Atman*. To live in solitude means to withdraw the mind from the outside world. One can live in solitude and by oneself even in the midst of the bazaar in Ahmedabad [the city adjacent to Satyagraha Ashram]. Even so, one must also have physical solitude. One can go to a cremation ground and, thinking on the perishable body, experience the feeling of solitude.

He who lives by himself and seeks to control his mind should shed all desires and, having renounced all possessions, yoke the *Atman* to the *Paramatman* in contemplation. Renunciation of possessions includes renunciation of the desire for possessions, too.

Can anyone, however, do without some possessions for the comfort of the body? We should supply the body its minimum needs and not seek to multiply them. If we go on multiplying bodily needs, we shall ever be going from birth to death and from death to birth. So long as the turban is there, we may use it, but we should not buy another to replace it. Likewise, we may look after the body, but only to supply its minimum needs. We shall not then have to be born and to die again and again.

(11) Fixing for himself, in a pure spot, a firm seat, neither too high nor yet too low, covered with kasha grass, thereon a deerskin and thereon a cloth,

(12) Sitting on that seat, with mind concentrated, the functions of thought and sense in control, he should set himself to the practice of *yoga* for the sake of self-purification.

(13) Keeping himself steady, holding the trunk, the neck and the head in a straight line and motionless, fixing his eye on the tip of his nose, and looking, not around;

(14) Tranquil in spirit, free from fear, steadfast in the vow of *Brahmacharya* (self-control), holding his mind in control, the *yogi* should sit, with all his thoughts on Me, absorbed in Me.

These four verses describe processes of *yoga*. I remember to have read in jail that they would take not less than six months to learn. These processes are physical actions, and we cannot be certain that everyone will profit from them. The body and the mind, however, are so difficult to control that, in our country, people attach special importance to these processes.

When such ideas are given importance in theory, all kinds of experiments are undertaken. Two Italian boys had decided to tour round the whole earth walking. They were just young boys. They were happy with what they had undertaken. When I asked them what they hoped to learn from their tour, one of them got very angry. They would acquire a venturesome spirit from which they themselves would profit, but in other ways they would have simply thrown away their lives.

The same is true about *pranayama* (a *yogic* practice involving the breath) and other processes which have been mentioned; but there is no fraud behind them, and no intention to impose on people. They are a means of fixing our mind on God.

(15) The *yogi* who, ever thus, with mind controlled, unites himself to *Atman* wins the peace which culminates in *nirvana*, the peace that is in Me.

(16) *Yoga* is not for him who eats too much, nor for him who fasts too much, neither for him who sleeps too much, nor yet for him who is too wakeful.

This is said in continuation of the preceding four verses. It is true that anyone who eats or sleeps too much can achieve nothing. Some persons live merely on the physical level. They can achieve nothing worth while; but the converse requires a little thinking about. He who has undertaken spiritual discipline and eats too little will not be able to provide his *chitta* (empirical mind) the nourishment it needs and so he will not succeed in fixing his thoughts on God. And the same is true about keeping awake.

There is no fear that anyone here intends to abstain from food or to keep awake too long in this manner. This verse refers to a person who imposes such discipline on himself for progress in *yoga*; but a person who, however hard he tries, cannot acquire control over his senses, whose eyes always open to cast lustful glances and whose other senses, too, crave indulgence — let such a person certainly undertake long fasts, even if his body should perish in consequence.

Any of us here may fast if he feels that he cannot curb his cravings in any other way. An idea has come to prevail nowadays that in this world one must satisfy one's desires. Hence my advice to you that you should not spare yourself any harshness in striving for self-purification. If a person loves to boast about secretly gratifying his eye, ear or palate, it would do him much good to take any number of vows to curb the body and cultivate vigilance.

The verses we have just discussed describe a method which serves as a help like that with which a child may learn to walk. They advise one to follow the golden mean. A time may come, however, when we shall not feel as excess what may seem to be so to an ordinary person. When we are distracted by innumerable evil impulses and feel ourselves helpless to curb them, we must begin by noncooperating with the evil impulses in our heart. We must tell the body that we have been paying it hire in the form of food for working as our watchman, but that we have decided to stop paying it from today because it is not doing its duty properly. We may pay rent only for a house which serves to protect us, of which the roof does not leak and the walls are not dilapidated. Why pay for a house which is rotten inside?

(17) To him who is disciplined in food and recreation, in effort in all activities, and in sleep and waking, *yoga* (discipline) becomes a relief from all ills.

(18) When one's thought, completely controlled, rests steadily only on *Atman*, when one is free from longing for all objects of desire, then one is called a *yogi*.

(19) As a taper in a windless spot flickers not, even so is a *yogi*, with his thought controlled, seeking to unite himself with *Atman*.

(20) Where thought curbed by the practice of *yoga* completely ceases, where a man sits content within himself, *Atman* having seen *Atman*;

"*Atman* having seen *Atman*," that is, when his mind has become absorbed in the *Atman* and he lives for ever content in the *Atman*.

(21) Where he experiences that endless bliss beyond the senses, which can be grasped by reason alone, wherein established he swerves not from the Truth;

If a person has perceived with his intellect the reality which God is, if he has understood with it his duty and then yoked himself to the chariot of God, if, shaking off lethargy, he has entered his name in God's office for duty — such a person will never be shaken from his purpose.

(22) Where he holds no other gain greater than that which he has gained, and where, securely seated, he is not shaken by any calamity however great —

Such a condition is possible only if one thinks about nothing but *Ramanama* (God's name) even in one's dreams, if one has worked the whole day in a disinterested spirit of service. If we have not spent the night in sound sleep, if we have had a bad dream, we may understand that our mind is still full of greed, attachment, etc.

(23) That state should be known as *yoga* (union with the Supreme), the disunion from all union with pain. This *yoga* must one practice with firm resolve and unwearying zeal.

Anyone who depends for his happiness on external circumstances makes it plain that, in fact, he does not want to be happy. In the end such a person becomes unhappy. Happiness and misery — we should throw both into the river Sabarmati. He who rises above both happiness and misery has achieved *yoga*. *Yoga* means absence of suffering, never feeling miserable. If anyone abuses us, we should lay the abuse at God's feet. Likewise, if anyone praises us, the praise, too, we should lay at His feet. This is the meaning of nonpossessiveness. He is a *yogi* who cultivates such a state of mind and feels himself as light as a flower.

(24) Shaking oneself completely free from longings born of selfish purpose, reining in the whole host of senses from all sides with the mind itself,

(25) With reason held securely by the will, he should gradually attain calm, and with the mind established in *Atman* think of nothing.

(26) Wherever the fickle and unsteady mind wanders, thence should it be reined in and brought under the sole sway of *Atman*.

The speed of air can be measured by a meteorologist and that of electricity by a scientist; but no machine has yet been invented to measure the speed of the mind. It is unsteady and restless. We should withdraw it from every direction in which it flies and fix it in the right place, that is, in the *Atman*.

(27) For supreme bliss comes to this *yogi*, who, with mind becalmed, with passions stilled, has become one with *Brahman*, and is purged of all stain.

(28) The *yogi*, cleansed of all stain, unites himself ever thus to *Atman* and easily enjoys the endless bliss of contact with *Brahman*.

(29) The man equipped with *yoga* looks on all with an impartial eye, seeing *Atman* in all beings and all beings in *Atman*.

The *yogi* is not one who sits down to practice breathing exercises. He is one who looks upon all with an equal eye, sees other creatures in himself. Such a one attains *moksha*. To look upon all with an equal eye means to act towards others as we would towards ourselves. That idea is explained still further in the following verse.

(30) He who sees Me everywhere and everything in Me, never vanishes from Me nor I from him.

It is not easy to see all creatures in ourselves. The key with which to achieve this is given in the next verse, and that is, that one should see others in oneself by seeing them and oneself in God. As ice becomes what it is from water, so we have all come from the same water and shall turn again into that water. The hailstone which realizes that it is water in substance will feel itself as water. God and God's *maya* [visible creation] are one.

(31) The *yogi* who, anchored in unity, worships Me abiding in all beings lives and moves in Me, no matter how he live and move.

(32) He who, by likening himself with others, senses pleasure and pain equally for all as for himself is deemed to be the highest *yogi*, O Arjuna.

He who acts towards others as if they were himself will meet their needs as if they were his own, will do to others what he would to himself, will learn to look upon himself and the world as one. He is a true *yogi* who is happy when others are happy and suffers when others suffer.

Only that person who has reduced himself to a cipher, has completely shed his egotism, can claim to be so. He alone may be said to be such a person who has dedicated his all to God; but this is a difficult state to achieve, and so Arjuna puts a question.

Arjuna said:

(33) I do not see, O Madhusudana, how this *yoga*, based on the equal-mindedness that Thou hast expounded to me, can steadily endure, because of fickleness (of the mind).

(34) For fickle is the mind, O Krishna, unruly, overpowering and stubborn. To curb it is, I think, as hard as to curb the wind.

The Lord said:

(35) Undoubtedly, O Mahabahu, the mind is fickle and hard to curb; yet, O Kaunteya, it can be held in check by constant practice and dispassion.

(36) Without self-restraint, *yoga*, I hold, is difficult to attain; but the self-governed soul can attain it by proper means, if he strive for it.

Arjuna has became a bridge between Shri Krishna and the world. Possessing such knowledge, and after having enjoyed the privilege of Shri Krishna's company for so long a time, he should have no question to ask. It is for the benefit of the world that he puts all his questions.

Arjuna said:

(37) If one, possessed of faith but slack of effort, because of his mind straying from *yoga*, reach not perfection in *yoga*, what end does he come to, O Krishna?

(38) Without a foothold, and floundering in the path to *Brahman*, fallen from both, is he indeed not lost, O Mahabahu, like a dissipated cloud?

(39) This my doubt, O Krishna, do Thou dispel utterly; for there is to be found none other than Thou to banish this doubt

The Lord said:

(40) Neither in this world nor in the next can there be ruin for him, O Partha. No well-doer, O loved one, meets with a sad end.

In these words, Shri Krishna assures the whole world that He will always welcome those who seek Him as persons engaged in a good effort, no matter with what energy they pursue their aim. Every action bears fruit and in particular no effort for realizing God is ever wasted. A person making such an effort never falls, but always rises. If he has faith, what does it matter if he cannot strive with determination? Whatever his achievement, he will be counted as a soldier in God's army.

(41) Fallen from *yoga*, a man attains the world of righteous souls, and, having dwelt there for numberless years, is then born to a house of pure and gentle blood.

Such a person rises, after his death, to the world which men of good deeds attain and, after dwelling in it for a long time, is born in a family of men who are holy and possess *shri* — that is, men who enjoy God's grace, not necessarily possess riches, for it is difficult for one born in a rich family to practice *yoga* or chant *Ramanama*.

(42) Or he may even be born into a family of *yogis*, though such birth as this is all too rare in this world.

(43) There, O Kurunandana, he recovers the intellectual stage he had reached in his previous birth, and thence he stretches forward again towards perfection.

He acquires in this life the state which he had failed to acquire in his previous life, whether or not he remembers his effort in that life. If a boy of eight can look upon all with equal regard, we shall conclude that that is the effect of his mode of life in a previous birth. He will then strive further in the same direction and ultimately reach his goal.

(44) By virtue of that previous practice he is borne on, whether he will it or not. Even he with a desire to know *yoga* passes beyond the Vedic ritual.

That is, he goes beyond the endless forms of *karma* and rituals enjoined in the Vedas, not beyond the *karma* which we undertake with a view to service or in a disinterested spirit.

(45) But the *yogi* who perseveres in his striving, cleansed of sin, perfected through many births, reaches the highest state.

The capital of self-purification acquired in this life will never be wasted. Persevering in his effort, such a *yogi* destroys the effects of his sins and, succeeding in his aim after many lives, attains *moksha*.

(46) The *yogi* is deemed higher than the man of austerities. He is deemed also higher than the man of knowledge. Higher is he than the man engrossed in ritual; therefore be thou a *yogi*, O Arjuna.

The man of austerities means the man practicing them with an eye to the fruit. The man of knowledge does not mean the *jnani* who has realized the truth, but a man of learning.

(47) And among all *yogis*, he who worships Me with faith, his inmost self all rapt in Me, is deemed by Me to be the best *yogi*.

Among all classes of *yogis*, the best, of course, is the one who has faith in God. As the rays of the moon are the only thing which will make the chataka bird happy, so nothing is as effective as constant repetition of the Lord's name for ending man's suffering in this world.

In this sixth chapter, Shri Krishna has explained how one may cultivate the spirit of sacrifice through work. He has explained the means of learning self-control. As the method, however, is difficult to practice — and it is not essential that everyone should follow it — the question is raised whether a person who fails in such an effort does not get the worst of both the worlds. Replying, Shri Krishna says, "No. Nothing done with a spiritual motive is lost."

Hatha yogis [practitioners of *yoga* in its primarily physical aspect] believe chapter six to have been written for them. Their belief is that it was written because *hatha yoga* has a place in the practice of *yoga*. I do not share this view, though I admit that *hatha yoga* has some utility. We should avail ourselves of all possible means which help in realization.

It is said about the purely physical processes described in *hatha yoga* that those who go through them will attain self-realization; but these processes do not necessarily take one to God. The secret of rising towards God lies in the mind. Anyone who practices these processes, knowing that they help control of the mind, will certainly derive much profit from them. We have not taken them up because we have not met anyone who knows them. We have been visited by many who believed in them and recommended them to us, but none who knew them. Hence I have done nothing in that field; but I do have them in my mind. I mention this thing so that, if you come across a *sadhu* who is like me a seeker, you should avail yourselves of his services.

Chapter Seven

The Lord said:

(1) Hear, O Partha, how, with thy mind riveted on Me, by practicing *yoga* and making Me the sole refuge, thou shalt, without doubt, know Me fully.

(2) I will declare to thee, in its entirety, this knowledge [*jnana*], combined with discriminative knowledge [*vijnana*], which when thou hast known there remains here nothing more to be known.

(3) Among thousands of men hardly one strives after perfection. Among those who strive hardly one knows Me in truth.

(4) Earth, Water, Fire, Air, Ether, Mind, Reason and Ego — thus eightfold is my *prakriti* [the primary substance of the material world] divided.

(5) This is My lower aspect; but know thou My other aspect, the higher — which is *jiva* [the vital essence, soul] by which, O Mahabahu, this world is sustained.

Shri Krishna says to Arjuna, "There is also another *prakriti* of Mine which you may call *paraprakriti*. It exists in living creatures, and is superior to the *prakriti* in inert matter. Through it the entire universe exists."

[Upon being told that some of the young devotees had killed a snake:] This is a difficult matter. We may catch a snake and remove it, but should do so gently. We should not inflict pain on it. We should think on this matter not because someone wants us to do so, but because we want to put the teaching of the Gita into practice. We should certainly not beat up a snake for our pleasure. This is ignorance and cruelty. Even a child should think how he or she would feel if someone treated him or her in the same manner.

Do not tell yourselves that you will think about these matters when you have white hair on your heads. You must make the best use of your youth right now. As Lord Krishna said, among thousands only one person strives for self-realization, that is, for self-purification, and among the thousands who strive only a rare person comes to a right knowledge of Him. Hence we should strive hard and long. We should look upon ourselves as those exceptional persons among thousands. We should try to become philosophers. We should aspire to be the rare individuals among those thousands, and hope that we shall succeed.

(6) Know that these two compose the source from which all beings spring. I am the origin and end of the entire universe.

(7) There is nothing higher than I, O Dhananjaya. All this is strung on Me as a row of gems upon a thread.

(8) In water I am the savor, O Kaunteya. In the sun and the moon I am the light; the syllable "Aum" in all the Vedas; the sound in ether, and manliness in men.

(9) I am the sweet fragrance in earth; the brilliance in fire; the life in all beings; and the austerity in ascetics.

(10) Know Me, O Partha, to be the primeval seed of all beings. I am the reason of rational beings and the splendor of the splendid.

(11) Of the strong, I am the strength, divorced from lust and passion. In beings I am *kama* [desire] undivorced from *dharma* [righteousness].

"*Kama* undivorced from *dharma*" means the desire for *moksha*, or the desire to end the suffering of creatures. If we desire to end the suffering of others, our suffering, too, will end. In Sanskrit the desire to end the suffering of others is described as *mahaswartha*, supreme self-interest. It means interest in the *moksha*, of all creatures. Anyone who feels such a desire would be striving hard for his own *moksha*.

(12) Know that all the manifestations of the three *gunas* — *sattva, rajas,* and *tamas* — proceed from none but Me; yet I am not in them. They are in Me.

We say that we should offer up everything to God, even evil. The two — good and evil — are inseparable, and so we should offer up both. If we wish to give up sin, we should give up virtue too. There is possessiveness in clinging even to virtue.

(13) Befogged by these manifestations of the three *gunas,* the entire world fails to recognize Me, the imperishable, as transcending them.

Truly speaking, even those who are ruled by *sattvic* impulses may be said to be under their [the *gunas'*] power because of their ignorance.

(14) For this My divine delusive mystery made up of the three *gunas* is hard to pierce; but those who make Me their sole refuge pierce the veil.

(15) The deluded evildoers, lowest of men, do not seek refuge in Me; for, by reason of this delusive mystery, they are bereft of knowledge and given to devilish ways.

(16) Four types of well-doers are devoted to Me, O Arjuna. They are, O Bharatarshabha, the afflicted, the spiritual seeker, the material seeker, and the enlightened.

My worshippers whose actions are ever the holiest fall into four classes, says Shri Krishna. They are, (1) those in distress, (2) those who yearn for true knowledge or seek *moksha*, (3) those who worship Me for worldly benefits, and (4) the *jnanis*, the enlightened, who worship God as His servants and seek nothing from Him. The latter tell God that it was simply their duty, as His subjects, to worship Him, and that it made no difference to them whether or not He rewarded them.

(17) Of these the enlightened, ever attached to Me in single-minded devotion, is the best; for to the enlightened I am exceedingly dear and he is dear to Me.

Shri Krishna says, "Among them all, the *jnani*, who always lives in union with Me, yoked with Me, who calls upon Me, 'Thou, thou,' who lives as a devotee, and keeps repeating My name is the best. I am very dear to such *jnanis* and they to Me. We are thus like the lover and the beloved."

(18) All these are estimable indeed, but the enlightened I hold to be My very self; for he, the true *yogi*, is stayed on Me alone, the supreme goal.

(19) At the end of many births the enlightened man finds refuge in Me. Rare indeed is this great soul to whom Vasudeva [Krishna] is all.

"At the end of many births" means after a long and hard struggle. Such a person is always saying, not with his tongue merely but with his very heart, that this whole universe is a manifestation of Vasudeva. A *mahatma* of that greatness is very rare.

(20) Men, bereft of knowledge by reason of various longings, seek refuge in other gods, pinning their faith on diverse rites, guided by their own nature.

Some, for instance, vow to make a gift of so much rice or so many coconuts to the Mother-goddess at Khodiar. They obey their nature and worship her in that manner.

(21) Whatever form one desires to worship in faith and devotion, in that very form I make that faith of his secure.

(22) Possessed of that faith he seeks to propitiate that one, and obtains therethrough his longings, dispensed in truth by none but Me.

(23) But limited is the fruit that falls to those shortsighted ones. Those who worship the gods go to the gods, those who worship Me come unto Me.

Shortsighted worshippers of gods reap perishable fruits. Only one type of person wins deliverance. Those who worship the lower gods rise so far as the world of those gods. "Those who worship Me," Krishna says, "come direct to Me."

(24) Not knowing My transcendent, imperishable, supreme character, the undiscerning think Me who am unmanifest to have become manifest.

"These persons of little intelligence do not know My unmanifest state," says Shri Krishna. "They mistake the manifest universe for the invisible reality behind. They do not know the best part of Me at all (the part beyond the manifest), do not know Me as the changeless, supreme Purushottama."

If, for instance, we worship the Sun, who gives light and heat, we divide the divine power of God into several aspects and worship one of them. Instead, we should try to know the highest, the invisible state of God. This visible universe is ever taking new shades. The gods change their forms but God is ever the same.

(25) Veiled by the delusive mystery created by My unique power, I am not manifest to all. This bewildered world does not recognize Me, birthless and changeless.

If someone told us that in his country rivers freeze and that human beings and vehicles can pass over them, we would not easily understand his statement. This idea of Reality veiled behind these objects with name and form is similar to that. It is true, nonetheless. The Lord says that this is due to the power of

His *yogamaya* [creative power], that His real essence is the Unmanifest.

But, then, one may ask, why did God create this universe at all? To ask this question is like a clock asking why its maker made it. A creature must have complete faith in its creator.

(26) I know, O Arjuna, all creatures past, present and to be; but no one knows Me.

(27) All creatures in this universe are bewildered, O Parantapa, by virtue of the delusion of the pairs of opposites sprung from likes and dislikes, O Bharata.

(28) But those virtuous men whose sin has come to an end, freed from the delusion of the pairs of opposites, worship Me in steadfast faith.

(29) Those who endeavor for freedom from age and death by taking refuge in Me know, in full, that *Brahman*, *adhyatma* and all *karma*.

(30) Those who know Me — including *adhibhuta*, *adhidaiva*, *adhiyajna* — possessed of even-mindedness, they know Me even at the time of passing away.

The terms in italics are defined in the next chapter. The sense is that every nook and cranny of the universe is filled with *Brahman*, that He is the sole agent of all action, and that the man who, imbued with this knowledge and faith, completely surrenders himself to Him, becomes one with Him at the time of passing hence. All his desires are extinguished in this vision of Him and he wins his freedom.

Chapter Eight

The main question raised in chapter one was, how can one kill one's kinsmen? The answer to this extended to seven chapters. And now begins the eighth. Shri Krishna is making all this effort with the aim of removing the confusion of thought and the ignorance which had unsettled Arjuna's mind. He has been brought to the point of distinction between the *apara prakriti*, the world of visible objects, and the *para prakriti*, which can be apprehended only when we go beyond the senses, the intellect and the ego.

Arjuna said:

(1) What is the *Brahman*? What is *adhyatma*? What *karma*, O Purushottama? What is called *adhibhuta*? And what *adhidaiva*?

(2) And who here in this body is *adhiyajna* and how? And how at the time of death art Thou to be known by the self-controlled?

The Lord said:

(3) The Supreme, the Imperishable is *Brahman*. Its manifestation is *adhyatma*. The creative process whereby all beings are created is called *karma*.

(4) *Adhibhuta* is My perishable form. *Adhidaiva* is the individual self in that form; and, O best among the embodied, *adhiyajna* am I in this body, purified by sacrifice.

That which never perishes and is the ultimate Reality is *Brahman*. Our nature is *adhyatma*. Creating all beings and keeping them in existence is an act of renunciation and is known as *karma*. The modes of being which belong to the living creatures in the world are perishable modes. Shri Krishna is the Lord of *yajnas* and grants their fruit.

That is, from Imperishable Unmanifest down to the perishable atom everything in the universe is the Supreme and an expression of the Supreme. Why, then, should mortal man arrogate to himself authorship of anything rather than do His bidding and dedicate all action to Him?

(5) And he who, at the last hour remembering Me only, departs leaving the body, enters into Me; of that there is no doubt.

(6) Or whatever form a man continually contemplates, that same he remembers in the hour of death, and to that very form he goes, O Kaunteya.

Shri Krishna has packed in these two verses the essence of all philosophy: man will reap as he thinks.

We should let no impurity enter our thoughts. Parents give us the human form, sometimes a form like their own. The subtle changes which take place within us become visible through our eyes. If we get a disease, we should believe that we ourselves are the cause of it. A person whose mind is so strong that he influences his surroundings instead of being influenced by them gets no disease. It is for our good, therefore, to believe that our illness is the result of our sins.

If we have been repeating *Ramanama* [God's name] from the depth of our heart, how can even a dream, if it is evil, leap over that protecting wall and enter our mind? If any does, we may believe that we have been uttering *Ramanama* only with our lips. If we have any fear whatever in our heart, that too is a form of evil and we suffer from many serious diseases because of it. Hence, as we free ourselves more and more from evil impulses and desires, we become less and less subject to disease.

Even persons whose ears and noses and all other limbs had been infected are known to have recovered. The body possesses a natural power of recovery. Recovery brought about with the help of herbs lasts for some time only. The man who has overcome his evil desires and cultivated devotion to God will refuse to be cured with the help of herbs. He will say that, when the evil in him has disappeared, he will be all right. If, as a result of this attitude, he dies, he will welcome death.

Anyone who thinks wicked thoughts will find that one day his body has become ugly. Once a person charged with murder came to me. I merely looked at him and told him that he was trying to deceive me. He left at once.

(7) Therefore at all times remember Me and fight on. Thy mind and reason thus on Me fixed, thou shalt surely come to me.

(8) With thought steadied by constant practice, and wandering nowhere, he who meditates on the Supreme Celestial Being, O Partha, goes to Him.

No one should believe that it will suffice if he does this at the moment of death. He who has been striving in this direction from his childhood will win the battle and the other will lose.

(9-10) Who, at the time of death, with unwavering mind, with devotion, and fixing the breath rightly between the brows by the power of *yoga*, meditates on the Sage, the Ancient, the Ruler, Subtler than the subtlest, the Supporter of all, the Inconceivable, Glorious as the Sun beyond the darkness — he goes to that Supreme Celestial Being.

At the moment of departing, that is, when dying, one should think on that *Purusha* [soul] Who is beginningless, Who rules the world, and Who is, in essence, finer than the finest we can conceive.

In the sixth century B.C., there ruled in Lydia a king named Croesus. He had immense wealth. The Greek saint and lawgiver, Solon, once went to see him. Croesus asked him whether anyone could be happier than he himself was. Solon's reply was that only after a man has died can we say whether he had been happy. This same Croesus was afterwards attacked and defeated by King Cyrus of Persia. He was sentenced to be hanged. As he was being taken to the gallows, he shouted Solon's name thrice. On being asked by Cyrus why he did that, he repeated Solon's reply to his question. Cyrus freed him and kept him as his adviser. When the King died, he left his son in the care of Croesus. In much the same way, it is only after a man's death that we can say whether he has passed into a higher world.

Proceeding, Shri Krishna describes that supreme *Purusha*. He who, when leaving this world, thinks with a fixed mind on this *Purusha* — only his mind is fixed who has yoked himself to the Lord in devotion and who possesses the strength acquired by long discipline — thinks of Him with devotion and with the power of his *yoga*, who refuses any treatment or medicine to save his life, who knows that he is leaving for a world where there is no darkness and no suffering or happiness, and who focuses his *prana* [vital energy] on the point midway between his brows and meditates — such a person attains to the realm of the Supreme, the Divine *Purusha* described in this verse.

(11) That which the knowers of the Vedas call the Imperishable, wherein the ascetics, freed from passion, enter and, desiring which they practice self-control, that Goal (or Word) I will declare to thee in brief.

(12) Closing all the gates, locking up the mind in the *hridaya* [heart], fixing his breath within the head, rapt in *yogic* meditation,

(13) Who so departs leaving the body uttering "Aum" — *Brahman* in one syllable — repeatedly thinking on Me, he reaches the highest state.

(14) That *yogi* easily comes to Me, O Partha, who, ever attached to Me, constantly remembers Me with undivided mind.

(15) Great souls, having come to Me, reach the highest perfection. They come not again to birth, unlasting and (withal) an abode of misery.

It is not because the Gita says so that we should regard life and death as the cause of suffering. We should feel in our own lives that they are so. The best way of ensuring that after death we pass to a higher world is to feel every moment that life in this world is from its very nature full of suffering, so that we give up attachment to it and free ourselves from the dualities of love and hatred.

We can understand even with our reason that life in this world is full of suffering. If we but think, we shall realize that the very process of birth of all creatures is something repulsive, and our state after birth is, from the beginning to the end, one long imprisonment. We take pleasure in this slavery because it is a part of our existence, but in truth it is a state in which we cannot rest in peace even for a moment.

Even then, this prison is a house through which we can win our freedom. If we come to regard it in that light, we shall make the minimum necessary use of it.

The supreme state to which He shall raise us is not to be conceived as one in which a higher bliss we may experience in this life will vanish. On the contrary, we shall have it thousand-fold in that other state. With this thought constantly in one's mind, one should get absorbed in the duties of this life, forget oneself altogether in them. One should see oneself in the whole world and the whole world in oneself, and act toward others accordingly. The ideal of nonviolence had its origin in this realization — that when human life is full of suffering, we should cause suffering to none.

(16) From the world of Brahma down, all the worlds are subject to return, O Arjuna; but on coming to Me there is no rebirth.

All the worlds, including the world of Brahma [the creator God in the Hindu trinity], will return to their source. The sun, the moon, Brahma, Vishnu, all will perish. "But," Shri Krishna says, "once a human being comes to Me, he never perishes."

There is great poetry in this verse. This little drop contains knowledge as vast as the sea, and the more that knowledge becomes part of our experience the more we discover its poetry. In such a verse, the poet soars on the wings of his imagination, released from the bondage of the body and the senses. His imagination works on what he has heard with his ears and seen with his eyes and, going beyond the certainties of reason, he says that all that is known through the senses is a product of the human mind. That is, he imagines that since we ourselves perish, this whole universe will perish too. All that the human mind can imagine or conceive is perishable, is subject to ceaseless change.

Shri Krishna, therefore, the Prince of *Yogis* that He is, says here that we believe there is happiness in the world of Brahma but that there is no happiness even there. He asks Arjuna to go to the world beyond all these worlds, the world in which He Himself dwells. This is simply beyond our imagination; but what is beyond our imagination does exist, nevertheless. If a person dies striving to reach that world, there is no rebirth for him.

(17) Those men indeed know what is day and what is night, who know that Brahma's day lasts a thousand *yugas* [ages] and that his night too is a thousand *yugas* long.

That is to say, our day and night of a dozen hours each are less than the infinitesimal fraction of a moment in that vast cycle of time. Pleasures pursued during these incalculably small moments are as illusory as a mirage. Rather than waste these brief moments, we should devote them to serving God through the service of mankind. On the other hand, our time is such a small drop in the ocean of eternity that if we fail of our object here, viz. self-realization, we need not despair. We should bide our time.

(18) At the coming of day all the Manifest spring forth from the Unmanifest, and at the coming of night they are dissolved into that same Unmanifest.

All creation appears and vanishes, and does so endlessly. Knowing this, man should understand that he has very little power over things. The round of birth and death is ceaseless.

(19) This same multitude of creatures comes to birth, O Partha, again and again. They are dissolved at the coming of night, whether they will or not, and at the break of day they are reborn.

(20) But higher than that Unmanifest is another Unmanifest Being, everlasting, which perisheth not when all creatures perish.

There is another Unmanifest Reality beyond this Unmanifest and it is immutable. It is the immutable Reality immanent in all perishable creatures. Everything which exists will perish, but the ground of all this existence is imperishable.

(21) This Unmanifest, named the Imperishable, is declared to be the highest goal. For those who reach it there is no return. That is My highest abode.

Shri Krishna says, "You can come to Me by patient striving and by living in this world only as a witness. Have faith and, devoting yourself to duty, work out the welfare of your soul." The substance of all this is that the supreme *Brahman* never perishes, everything else does.

---

(22) This Supreme Being, O Partha, may be won by undivided devotion. In It all beings dwell. By It all is pervaded.

(23) Now I will tell thee, Bharatarshabha, the conditions which determine the exemption from return, as also the return, of *yogis* after they pass away hence.

(24) Fire, light, day, the bright fortnight, the six months of the Northern Solstice — through these departing men knowing *Brahman* go to *Brahman*.

(25) Smoke, night, the dark fortnight, the six months of the Southern Solstice — therethrough the *yogi* attains to the lunar light and thence returns.

I do not understand the meaning of these last two verses. They do not seem to me to be consistent with the teaching of the Gita. The Gita teaches that he whose heart is meek with devotion, who is devoted to unattached action and has seen the Truth must win salvation, no matter when he dies. These verses seem to run counter to this. They may perhaps be stretched to mean broadly that a man of sacrifice, a man of light, a man who has known *Brahman*, finds release from birth if he retains that enlightenment at the time of death. On the contrary the man who has none of these attributes goes to the world of the moon — not at all lasting — and returns to birth. The moon, after all, shines with borrowed light.

(26) These two paths — bright and dark — are deemed to be the eternal paths of the world. By the one a man goes to return not, by the other he returns again.

The Bright one may be taken to mean the path of knowledge and the dark one that of ignorance.

(27) The *yogi* knowing these two paths falls not into delusion, O Partha; therefore, at all times, O Arjuna, remain steadfast in *yoga*.

The *yogi* who knows the distinction between these two paths never succumbs to darkness. He realizes that disinterested devotion is the best form of devotion. If we have faith in the Lord and devotion for Him, why should we forever be begging things from Him? Anyone who is filled with faith and love will feel that there is nothing for him to beg. He will have offered everything to the Lord, placed himself at His mercy. He may say, "All that is mine is yours." Such single-minded devotion is the Northern Solstice, it is light, and so on.

What, again, is the significance of Krishna's advice to "remain steadfast in yoga"? It means that one should cling to knowledge and single-minded devotion to Him. The gods are immortal, but only compared to human beings. They, too, will perish in time. "Therefore," says Shri Krishna, "instead of going to the gods who will perish, if you come to Me, then alone will you get knowledge and in no other way."

(28) Whatever fruit of good deeds is laid down as accruing from (a study of) the Vedas, from sacrifices, austerities, and acts of charity — all that the *yogi* transcends on knowing this, and reaches the Supreme and Primal Abode.

He who has acquired this light and knowledge has secured that beyond which nothing else remains to be obtained.

Chapter Nine

The Lord said:

(1) I will now declare to thee, who art uncensorious, this mysterious knowledge, together with discriminative knowledge, knowing which thou shalt be released from ill.

(2) This is the king of sciences, the king of mysteries, pure and sovereign, capable of direct comprehension, the essence of *dharma*, easy to practice, changeless.

Our first duty is service. The knowledge of this duty is *rajavidya*. It is the king of all secrets. It is sacred and the highest knowledge. It is *dharma* and worthy to be followed in action, and easy to follow besides. Once acquired, it is never destroyed. "I will impart that knowledge to you," says Shri Krishna.

(3) Men who have no faith in this doctrine, O Parantapa, far from coming to Me, return repeatedly to the path of this world of death.

(4) By Me, unmanifest in form, this whole world is pervaded. All beings are in Me. I am not in them.

(5) And yet those beings are not in Me. That indeed is My unique power as Lord. Sustainer of all beings, I am not in them. My Self brings them into existence.

The sovereign power of God lies in this mystery, this miracle, that all beings are in Him and yet not in Him, He in them and yet not in them. This is the description of God in the language of mortal man.

Indeed He soothes man by revealing to him all His aspects by using all kinds of paradoxes. All beings are in him inasmuch as all creation is His; but as He transcends it all, as He really is not the author of it all, it may be said with equal truth that the beings are not in Him. He really is in all His true devotees, He is not, according to them, in those who deny Him. What is this if not a mystery, a miracle of God?

(6) As the mighty wind, moving everywhere, is ever contained in ether, even so know that all beings are contained in Me.

Though space is empty, we can say that it is filled with air. And yet the air which fills space is still not in it. So God who dwells in all creatures is still not them. Ganges water does, and yet does not, contain dirt. Vyasa puts these contradictory statements together, for our reason knows its limitation in trying to describe the truth. It is enough if we understand that God pervades the entire universe.

God is omnipotent and we are His creatures. He is so near that we feel we can touch Him this very moment, and yet we never do, so far away He is. He who has faith certainly exists in God. He who lacks it does not. God does not force Himself on anyone, but He does not close the door, either, against anyone who aspires to be united to Him — such is His nature.

(7) All beings, O Kaunteya, merge into my *prakriti* [nature], at the end of a *kalpa* [cycle of time], and I send them forth again when a *kalpa* begins.

The individual soul passes through birth and death; but the universe, too, comes into existence and disappears. If the soul, therefore, wishes to know its essence, it will have to transcend the universe.

This ashram has buildings, which are its body, so to speak. They will be destroyed one day; but the ashram's soul, which is its ideals, will never perish. To realize its imperishable essence, we may need to put up buildings of brick and mortar. We must use our reason and discrimination and keep working. If we wish to live in this world, we must put to use even things which will perish, but only with the aim of realizing the imperishable essence beyond them.

(8) Resorting to my *prakriti*, I send forth again and again this multitude of beings, powerless under the sway of *prakriti*;

(9) But all this activity O Dhananjaya, does not bind Me, seated as one indifferent, unattached to it.

God acts according to His *prakriti*, and yet He does nothing since He is above even His *prakriti*.

It is man's nature to do good, for all selves are one. Man's essence, which is *Atman*, is all-pervading. He who has realized this will not see himself as different from others, but will see all in himself. For such a person, therefore, doing good becomes his nature. When he seems to be serving other creatures, he is doing so not out of kindness to them, but is merely following his own nature. To us who are enveloped in *maya*, it may seem that he is practising virtue, but in truth it is not so. He is acting only according to his nature towards all creatures.

(10) With me as presiding witness, *prakriti* gives birth to all that moves and does not move and, because of this, Kaunteya, the wheel of the world keeps going.

(11) Not knowing My transcendent nature as the sovereign Lord of all beings, fools condemn Me incarnated as man.

For they deny the existence of God and do not recognize the Director in the human body.

(12) Vain are the hopes, actions and knowledge of those witless ones who have resorted to the delusive nature of monsters and devils.

(13) But those great souls who resort to the divine nature, O Partha, know Me as the Imperishable Source of all beings and worship Me with an undivided mind.

"The *mahatmas* [great souls] who are ruled by their divine *prakriti* worship Me with their minds illumined by knowledge and with single-minded devotion — Me who am the Creator of all beings."

(14) Always declaring My glory, striving in steadfast faith, they do Me devout homage. Ever attached to Me, they worship Me.

(15) Yet others, with knowledge-sacrifice, worship Me, who am to be seen everywhere as one, as different or as many.

"Others worship Me by striving for knowledge. Some of them worship Me as the only One. Some others worship My different manifestations, and others still worship Me in everything which exists."

(16) I am the sacrificial vow. I am the sacrifice; I the ancestral oblation; I the herb; I the sacred text; I the clarified butter; I the fire; I the burnt offering.

(17) Of this universe I am Father, Mother, Creator, Grandsire. I am what is to be known, the sacred syllable "Aum", the Rig, the Sama and the Yajur [Vedas].

(18) I am the Goal, the Sustainer, the Lord, the Witness, the Abode, the Refuge, the Friend, the Origin, the End, the Preservation, the Treasure-house, the Imperishable Seed.

(19) I give heat. I hold back and pour forth rain. I am deathlessness and also death, O Arjuna, Being and Not-Being as well.

"I give heat, but in the form of the sun, which gives happiness and the light of knowledge to all creatures. I draw the rains and release them. I am death and I am immortality. I am Being and also Non-Being."

That is, every object and every state which we can think of in this universe are God. This means that God is not merely all that is good, He is also the evil. Nothing exists unless He wills it. It is not true that God is Lord of light and Satan of darkness. While we live in this body, we may believe in these dualities. We should engrave Tulsidasji's words in our hearts, that while we are enveloped in *maya,* all this, which is false, will seem as true. The alloy will appear as silver and the sun's rays will appear as the mirage. We shall continue to think in this way till a man of wisdom opens our eyes and convinces us that the appearance of the rope as serpent, of the alloy as silver and of the sun's rays as mirage, is but the work of our imagination.

We believe that God is both good and evil and, believing that, some of us ask what harm there is in following evil; but it is quite wrong if we argue thus. The point is not that we should act like scorpions or centipedes, but that we should have good-will for them, without ourselves becoming poisonous like them.

The Lord has here stated a profound truth which is beyond the capacity of our reason to comprehend. What He has stated cannot possibly be true in this world. We can only imagine that it must be true in some sense. Being and Non-Being, virtue and sin, immortality and death, these are contradictory things. They cannot be the same for human beings, they can be so only for God.

That third state (in which contraries are reconciled) is not a mere mixture of the two. Hydrogen and oxygen together yield water, but water does not display the separate properties of either. It has characteristics of it own. Similarly, we must not imagine that God has in Him the qualities of both virtue and sin, but should think that He has something else which is different from either. If we had both virtue and sin in us, there would be an explosion, but Siva swallows both. The existence of the two in God is a miracle, and He alone knows its mystery. We should make no attempt to cultivate such a state. If we try to combine the two in us, such an attempt to imitate God will simply destroy us.

(20) Followers of the three Vedas, who drink the soma juice and are purged of sin, worship Me with sacrifice and pray for going to heaven. They reach the holy world of the gods and enjoy in heaven the divine joys of the gods.

Those who perform the rituals enjoined in the three Vedas, who drink *somarasa*, who wash away their sins and worship the Lord by performing sacrifices, pray that they should go to heaven. They go to the sacred realm of Indra and there enjoy divine pleasures such as gods do.

(21 They enjoy the vast world of heaven, and, their merit spent, they enter the world of the mortals. Thus those who follow the Vedic law and long for the fruit of their action earn but the round of birth and death.

(22) As for those who worship Me, thinking on Me alone and nothing else, ever attached to Me, I bear the burden of getting them what they need.

(23) Even those who, devoted to other gods, worship them in full faith, even they, O Kaunteya, worship none but Me, though not according to the rule.

The right method is to have no intermediary between oneself and God. "But," Shri Krishna says, "those who seek Me through the gatekeepers that stand between, they too worship Me, for they worship these in order to reach Me."

(24) For I am the Acceptor and the Director of all sacrifices; but not recognizing Me as I am, they go astray.

"I am," says the Lord, "the recipient and the Lord of all *yajnas*." That is, he who does everything without thinking that he himself does it can say that not he but the Lord does everything. "Those, however, who do not know the truth and, therefore, do not know Me, return again to the world."

(25) Those who worship the gods go to the gods. Those who worship the *manes* [ancestors] go to the *manes*. Those who worship the spirits go to the spirits; but those who worship Me come to Me.

(26) Any offering of leaf, flower, fruit, or water made to Me in devotion by an earnest soul, I lovingly accept.

The Lord did not accept the fruit sent by Duryodhana, for he had not sent it with love. His motive was to get his own aim served through Shri Krishna. He wanted the Lord's help on his own terms. He had not mastered the self; but Vidura, who was a man of simple heart, offered a plain dish of leafy greens and the Lord accepted it with love, for Vidura's devotion was unrivaled and his heart was straightforward and clean. He felt no awe for the wealth of the mighty.

(27) Whatever thou dost, whatever thou eatest, whatever thou offerest as sacrifice or gift, whatever austerity thou dost perform, O Kaunteya, dedicate all to Me.

(28) So doing thou shalt be released from the bondage of action yielding good and evil fruit. Having accomplished both renunciation and performance, thou shalt be released (from birth and death) and come unto Me.

"If you live thus, you will be free from the bonds of *karma*, which are sometimes good sometimes evil in their fruit, for I shall be the recipient of all that you enjoy." He who has purified himself through renunciation — who dedicates to the Lord all that he does, who keeps on doing useful work right till the end of his life, but in a spirit of dedication to the Lord — such a one goes to Him after death.

(29) I am the same to all beings. With Me there is none disfavored, none favored; but those who worship Me with devotion are in Me and I in them.

(30) A sinner, howsoever great, if he turns to Me with undivided devotion, must indeed be counted a saint, for he has a settled resolve.

A man may have resolved to purify himself of the evil in him and he may sit down in a firm posture for *yoga*. Maybe his thoughts do not leave him, but he is nonetheless a saint who keeps repeating "Aum" and is firm in his resolution. Another person, who is not firm is his mind and not regular in practice, who follows no method in his work, may be a good man and still he does not deserve to be called a saint.

(31) For soon he becomes righteous and wins everlasting peace. Know for a certainty, O Kaunteya, that My devotee never perishes;

Such a person soon becomes a holy man, and attains inviolable peace of mind. We should not, therefore, regard even the most wicked of men as wicked. He can become good in this very life.

---

(32) For, finding refuge in Me, even those who though are born of the womb of sin — women, Vaisyas and Sudras — reach the supreme goal.

The Lord has given a great assurance to the world in these verses. This is His reply to those learned in the Vedas. Such persons argue that those who have not studied the Vedas cannot realize God. It was believed in those days that women, Vaisyas and Sudras [members of the two lower castes] cannot attain *moksha*. In fact, Krishna tended cows as a boy in Nanda's family and did the work of a Sudra. (The Vaisya's function was rearing cows and agriculture; but in course of time those who were engaged in agriculture came to be regarded as Sudras.) Shri Krishna says here that, even if Vaisyas and Sudras are not able to study the Vedas, they can certainly attain the blessed state. Anyone who, though ignorant of the Vedas, knows *Brahman* and has a pure heart is certain to attain this state.

(33) How much more then, the pure Brahmins and seer-kings who are my devotees? Do thou worship Me, therefore, since thou hast come to this fleeting and joyless world.

(34) On Me fix thy mind. To Me bring thy devotion. To Me offer thy sacrifice. To Me make thy obeisance. Thus having attached thyself to Me and made Me thy end and aim, to Me indeed shalt thou come.

This chapter has been named "The Sovereign Science" and "The *Yoga* of Sovereign Mystery." Shri Krishna tells Arjuna that He has explained the highest knowledge and expounded the highest mystery. The union of *yoga* is to be achieved with the

Lord. One should not aspire to earn great riches or rise to a position of honor or win an empire in this world. All that is needed is fixed determination to realize God.

What is the good of any pleasure we can get through the senses — the eyes, the nose, the ears and so on? We should not be allured by it, for such pleasure is short-lived. There were emperors, but they have passed away. He whom we seek dwells in our hearts, and the holy temple in which He sits opens only by the means of prayer.

The Lord explained this by saying "I am the author and sustainer of all. I am the friend. I am the source, the cause of existence and of the final destruction. I am all this. There is nothing else. I am all that there is. You are of no consequence. The other gods in the worlds in between will perish, like you. I alone never perish. If you wish that you should not perish, you should come to My world. That you can do by surrendering your whole mind to Me. Whether you are engaged in bathing or washing or any other like activities, if you are repeating my name the while, if you dedicate to Me all that you eat, and if you worship Me as you give your body its hire, you will surely come to Me."

Chapter Ten

The Lord said:

(1) Yet once more, O Mahabahu, hear My supreme word, which I will utter to thee, gratified one, for thy benefit.

(2) Neither the gods nor the great seers know My origin; for I am, every way, the origin of them both.

(3) He who knows Me, the great Lord of the worlds, as birthless and without beginning, he among mortals, undeluded, is released from sins.

"Those who know Me as the Unborn, the Beginningless and the Supreme Lord of all creatures do not sink into the darkness of ignorance."

A person who has sunk in darkness knows the night as day and the day as night. Among all these creatures who are bound to perish, the man of wisdom becomes free from all sins, for he will have no vestige of aversion and attachment, no trace of egotism. He will remain unaffected by the pairs of opposites, will ever be humble and believe that it is the Lord who provides for his living.

(4) Discernment, knowledge, freedom from delusion, long-suffering, truth, self-restraint, inward calm, pleasure, pain, birth, death, fear and fearlessness,

(5) Nonviolence, even-mindedness, contentment, auster-ity, beneficence, good and ill fame, — all these various attributes of creatures proceed verily from Me.

"All the qualities mentioned in these two verses — intel-lect, knowledge, the absence of ignorant attachment, forgive-ness, truthfulness, control of the senses, serenity, happiness and suffering, birth and death, fear and absence of fear, *ahimsa* [non-violence], inward poise and contentment, *tapas* [austerities], mak-ing gifts, good name or evil reputation among men — these conditions exist in all creatures and I am the cause of each one of them." The Creator of all beings is also the cause of all the good and evil which we see in these beings.

(6) The seven great seers, the ancient four, and the Manus, too, [the first men born in each age] were born of Me and of My mind, and of them were born all the creatures in the world.

(7) He who knows, in Truth, this My immanence and *yoga* becomes gifted with unshakable *yoga*; of this there is no doubt.

Everything which exists is created by the Lord. He who believes, not merely with his reason but with his heart, that no creature can live or act without His permission, or except as He wills, yokes himself to Him in single-minded devotion; but he who forgets the Lord and believes in his pride that he rises by his own efforts labors under a delusion. There is no doubt at all that he who believes in God from the depth of his heart and obeys the Lord who dwells in him attains to a state of serenity which is never perturbed.

———

(8) I am the source of all. All proceeds from Me. Knowing this, the wise worship Me with hearts full of devotion.

(9) With Me in their thoughts, their whole soul devoted to Me, teaching one another, with Me ever on their lips, they live in contentment and joy.

(10) To these, ever in tune with Me, worshipping Me with affectionate devotion, I give the power of selfless action, whereby they come to Me.

In this way knowledge comes spontaneously to a *bhakta*. He does not have to wade through big volumes; but he who believes that he will acquire knowledge first and cultivate *bhakti* afterwards will fail miserably in his aim. No one can acquire knowledge in that way. Such knowledge breeds, if anything, pride; but he who lovingly cultivates devotion for the Lord and constantly thinks on Him gets knowledge without any special effort to that end.

(11) Out of very compassion for them, I who dwell in their hearts, destroy the darkness, born of ignorance, with the refulgent lamp of knowledge.

Arjuna said:

(12) Lord, Thou art the supreme *Brahman*, the Supreme Abode, the Supreme Purifier, Everlasting Celestial Being, the Primal God, Unborn, All-pervading.

(13) Thus have all the seers — the divine seer Narada, Asita, Devala, Vyasa — declared Thee, and Thou Thyself dost tell me so.

(14) All that Thou tellest me is true, I know, O Keshava. Verily, Lord, neither the gods nor the demons know Thy manifestation.

(15) Thyself alone Thou knowest by Thyself, O Purushottama, Source and Lord of all beings, God of gods, O Ruler of the universe.

(16) Indeed, Thou oughtest to tell me of all Thy manifestations, without a remainder, whereby Thou dost pervade these worlds.

(17) O *Yogi*, constantly meditating on Thee, how am I to know Thee? In what various aspects am I to think of Thee, O Lord?

(18) Recount to me yet again, in full detail, Thy unique power and Thy immanence, O Janardana! For my ears cannot be sated with listening to Thy life-giving words.

One who does engraving work every day does not tire of it. He returns to it whenever he is free. Similarly, Arjuna, who loves repeating Krishna's name in devotion, requests Him again and again to describe His powers till the latter can say no more.

The Lord said:

(19) Yea, I will unfold to thee, O Kurushreshtha, My divine manifestation — the chiefest only; for there is no limit to their extent.

(20) I am the *Atman*, O Gudakesha, seated in the heart of every being. I am the beginning, the middle and the end of all beings.

---

(21) Of the Adityas I am Vishnu; of luminaries, the radiant Sun. Of Maruts I am Marichi; of constellations, the moon.

(22) Of the Vedas I am the Sama Veda; of the gods, Indra. Of the senses I am the mind. Of beings I am the consciousness.

(23) Of Rudras I am Shankara; of Yakshas and Rakshasas, Kubera. Of Vasus I am the Fire; of mountains, Meru.

(24) Of priests, O Partha, know Me to be the chief Brihaspati. Of army captains I am Kartikeya; and of waters, the ocean.

(25) Of the great seers I am Bhrigu. Of words I am the one syllable "Aum". Of sacrifices I am the Japa sacrifice; of things immovable, the Himalayas.

(26) Of all trees I am Ashvattha; of the divine seers, Narada. Of the heavenly choir I am Chitraratha. Of the perfected I am Kapila, the ascetic.

(27) Of horses, know Me to be Uchchaihshravas, born with *amrita*. Of mighty elephants I am Airavata; of men, the monarch.

(28) Of weapons I am Vajra; of cows, Kamadhenu. I am Kandarpa, the god of generation. Of serpents I am Vasuki.

(29) Of cobras I am Ananta. Of water-dwellers I am Varuna. Of the *manes* I am Aryaman; and of the chastisers, Yama.

(30) Of demons I am Prahlada; of reckoners, the Time. Of beasts I am the lion; and of birds, Garuda.

(31) Of cleansing agents I am the Wind; of wielders of weapons, Rama. Of fishes I am the crocodile; of rivers, the Ganges.

(32) Of creations I am the beginning, end and middle, O Arjuna; of sciences, the science of spiritual knowledge; of debaters, the right argument;

(33) Of letters, the letter A. Of compounds I am the *dvandva*. I am the imperishable Time. I am the creator to be seen everywhere.

(34) All-seizing Death am I, as also the source of things to be. In feminine virtues I am glory, beauty, speech, memory, intelligence, constancy and forgiveness.

(35) Of Saman hymns I am Brihat Saman; of metres, Gayatri. Of months I am the first; of seasons, the spring.

(36) Of deceivers I am the dice play; of the splendid, the splendor. I am victory. I am resolution. I am the goodness of the good.

"I am the gaming of those who indulge in gambling." This is merely intended to point out that God exists not only in what is good in the world, but also in what is evil. Shri Krishna could also have said that He was the sin of the wicked. The author's intention is only to assert that God is omnipotent. God's creation contains both good and evil. By saying this, Shri Krishna gives us some freedom to choose between the two. To us who are confined in the prison of this body, he grants that freedom. He gives us the freedom to shake off our bonds.

If a prisoner condemned to imprisonment for life is per-

mitted a seemingly unimportant condition by fulfilling which
he can be free, it will be a great thing for him, for he can secure
his freedom through it. We are in the same condition, for the
Lord has assured us that we can be what we wish to be.

(37) Of Vrishnis I am Vasudeva; of Pandavas, Dhananjaya.
Of ascetics I am Vyasa; and of seers, Ushanas.

(38) I am the rod of those that punish; the strategy of
those seeking victory. Of secret things I am silence, and
the knowledge of those that know.

(39) Whatever is the seed of every being, O Arjuna, that
am I. There is nothing, whether moving or fixed, that can
be without Me.

(40) There is no end to my divine manifestations. What
extent of them I have told thee now is only by way of
illustration.

(41) Whatever is glorious, beautiful and mighty, know
thou that all such has issued from a fragment of My splen-
dors.

(42) But why needst thou to learn this at great length, O
Arjuna? With but a part of Myself I stand upholding this
universe.

If we have an idea of the infinite powers of the Lord, we
shall become humble. The Lord has said that even being proud
is His privilege. The substance of all that He has said is that we
should learn to be the humblest of the humble. Knowing that
there is no limit to the power of God, we should submit to

violence if anyone attacks us, without offering violence in return. If we attempt to resist Him with violence, God will humble our pride; for there has been no demon whom the Lord has not destroyed.

Chapter Eleven

This is regarded as an important chapter. The Gita is a poem with a profound meaning, and the eleventh chapter is the most poetic of all. If we wish to learn true devotion, we should know this chapter by heart. If we do so, we shall feel, when reciting it, that we are bathing in a sea of devotion.

Arjuna said:

(1) Out of Thy grace towards me, Thou hast told me the supreme mystery revealing the knowledge of the Supreme; it has banished my delusion.

(2) Of the origin and destruction of beings I have heard from Thee in full detail, as also of Thy imperishable majesty, O Kamala-Patraksha.

(3) Thou art indeed just as Thou hast described Thyself, Parameshvara. I do crave to behold now that form of Thine as Ishvara.

(4) If, Lord, Thou thinkest it possible for me to bear the sight, reveal to me, O Yogeshvara, Thy imperishable form.

The Lord said:

(5) Behold, O Partha, my forms divine in their hundreds and thousands, infinitely diverse, infinitely various in color and aspect.

(6) Behold the Adityas, the Vasus, the Rudras, the two Ashwins, and the Maruts. Behold, O Bharata, numerous marvels never revealed before.

(7) Behold today, O Gudakesha, in my body, the whole universe moving and unmoving, all in one, and whatever else thou cravest to see.

"See the entire world, animate and inanimate, all as one reality." This cosmic form includes good and evil, Hindus and Muslims, believers and atheists, all.

(8) But thou canst not see Me with these thine own eyes. I give thee the eye divine. Behold My sovereign power!

Sanjaya said:

(9) With these words, O King, the great Lord of *Yoga*, Hari, then revealed to Partha His supreme form as Ishvara.

The teaching of the Gita was not meant to be merely preserved in a book. It was meant to be translated into action. Mahadev and Punjabhai take notes of what I speak, but had we arranged recording on a gramophone plate, every word could have been taken down. Could we have said, then, that the gramophone machine had understood the Gita? It is an inanimate object. Similarly, what will this knowledge profit us if we merely take down notes and do not put the teaching into practice?

(10) With many mouths, and many eyes, many wondrous aspects, many divine ornaments and many brandished weapons divine,

(11) Wearing divine garlands and vestments, anointed with divine perfumes, it was the form of God, all marvelous, infinite, seen everywhere.

(12) Were the splendor of a thousand suns to shoot forth all at once in the sky, that might perchance resemble the splendor of that Mighty One.

(13) Then did Pandava see the whole universe in its manifold divisions gathered as one in the body of that God of gods.

The whole universe, despite its manifold divisions, is gathered there in Him like a tree and its leaves. The tree is like the cosmic form of the Lord, the root and the leaves being one. The root contains the whole world of the tree, and the leaves represent that world divided into many forms. Arjuna saw thus the cosmic form of the God of gods.

(14) Then Dhananjaya, wonderstruck and thrilled in every fiber of his being, bowed low his head before the Lord, addressing Him thus with folded hands:

Arjuna said:

(15) Within Thy form, O Lord, I see all the gods and the diverse multitudes of beings, the Lord Brahma on his lotus-throne and all the seers and the serpents divine.

(16) With many arms and bellies, mouths and eyes, I see Thy infinite form everywhere. Neither Thy end, nor middle, nor beginning do I see, O Lord of the Universe, Universal formed!

On the one hand, Arjuna says that Shri Krishna has a definite form and, on the other, he says that He is formless. In other words, His form is so vast that in truth He is formless.

(17) With crown and mace and disc, a mass effulgence gleaming everywhere, I see Thee, so dazzling to the sight, bright with the splendor of the fiery sun blazing from all sides — incomprehensible.

The sun gives some faint idea of the Lord's light, but it is no more than a dim point of light in comparison with the Lord's.

(18) Thou art the Supreme Imperishable worthy to be known. Thou art the final resting place of this universe. Thou art the changeless guardian of the Eternal *Dharma*. Thou art, I believe, the Everlasting Being.

He has placed the sun at such a great distance from us. What would have been our condition if it had been a little nearer? Can we, then, imagine Arjuna's condition with Shri Krishna standing near him, Krishna glowing with the light of a thousand suns?

(19) Thou hast no beginning, middle nor end. Infinite is Thy might; arms innumerable; for eyes, the sun and the moon; Thy mouth a blazing fire, overpowering the universe with Thy radiance.

(20) By Thee alone are filled the spaces between heaven and earth and all the quarters. At the sight of this Thy wondrous terrible form, the three worlds are sore oppressed, O *Mahatman*.

(21) Here, too, the multitudes of gods are seen to enter Thee. Some, awestruck, praise Thee with folded arms. The hosts of great seers and saints, "All Hail" on their lips, hymn Thee with songs of Praise.

One feels as though these verses were specially written for us. We had information that there would be a heavy flood in the Sabarmati [River, running alongside the ashram]. Naturally, I was agitated in my heart, not knowing what to do; but I reminded myself of the verses which I daily recite before the women: "O Govind, dweller of Dwarika ... protector of Vraja, deliverer from affliction," and so on. Krishna would be welcome if he flew to our help. Otherwise, if all these things are carried away in the flood, our honor will still be saved. Let anyone who lives to witness the destruction live on faithful to our vows.

If the authorities of the Sabarmati jail invite us to take shelter in it, I will ask them if they have invited the people of Vadaj, too. I will tell them that they should offer shelter to all others before they invite us. Anyone who wishes to leave is certainly free to do so, either by train or to the city on the other side. As the headman of a village, this is all I can tell you. If you can think of anything better, please do.

(22) The Rudras, Adityas, Vasus, Sadhyas, all the gods, the twin Ashwins, Maruts, *manes*, the hosts of Gandharvas, Yakshas, Asuras and saints — all gaze on Thee in wonderment.

(23) At the sight of Thy mighty form, O Mahabahu, many-mouthed, with eyes, arms, thighs and feet innumerable, with many vast bellies, terrible with many jaws, the worlds feel fearfully oppressed, and so do I.

169

(24) For as I behold Thee touching the sky, glowing, numerous-hued, with gaping mouths and wide resplendent eyes, I feel oppressed in my innermost being. No peace nor quiet I find, O Vishnu!

(25) And as I see Thy mouths with fearful jaws, resembling the Fire of Doom, I lose all sense of direction, and find no relief. Be gracious, O Devesha, O Jagannivasa!

(26) All the sons of Dhritarashtra, and with them the crowd of kings — Bhisma, Drona, and that Karna too, as also our chief warriors —

(27) Are hastening into the fearful jaws of Thy terrible mouths. Some, indeed, caught between Thy teeth are seen, their heads being crushed to atoms.

(28) As rivers in their numerous torrents headlong to the sea, even so the heroes of the world of men rush into Thy flaming mouths.

(29) As moths, fast flying, plunge into blazing fire straight to their doom, even so these rush headlong into Thy mouths, to their destruction.

(30) Devouring all these from all sides, Thou lappest them with Thy flaming tongues. Thy fierce rays blaze forth, filling the whole universe with their luster.

(31) Tell me, Lord, who Thou art so dread of form. Hail to Thee, O Devavara! Be gracious! I desire to know Thee, Primal Lord; for I comprehend not what Thou dost.

The Lord said:

(32) Doom am I, full-ripe, dealing death to the worlds, engaged in devouring mankind. Even without thy slaying them, not one of the warriors ranged for battle against thee shall survive.

(33) Therefore, do thou arise, and win renown. Defeat thy foes and enjoy a thriving kingdom. By Me have these already been destroyed; be thou no more than an instrument, O Savyasachin.

"Savyasachin" means one who can use a bow with the left hand, that is, with either hand.

(34) Drona, Bhishma, Jayadratha and Karna, as also the other warrior chiefs — already slain by Me — slay thou! Be not dismayed. Fight! Victory is thine over thy foes in the field.

Sanjaya said:

(35) Hearing this word of Keshava, crown-wearer Arjuna folded his hands, and, trembling, made obeisance. Bowing and all hesitant, in faltering accents he proceeded to address Krishna once more.

Arjuna said:

(36) Right proper it is, O Hrishikesha, that Thy praise should stir the world to gladness and tender emotion. The Rakshasas in fear fly to every quarter and all the hosts of saints do reverent homage.

"And why should they not bow to you? You are the destroyer of the demons." The demons are our enemies, external and internal. What even if the river should swallow us and destroy us? How much more fearful is the flood inside us? Who will destroy the demons inside?

(37) And why should they not bow down to Thee, O *Mahatman*? Thou art the First Creator, greater even than Brahma. O Ananta, O Devesha, O Jagannivasa, Thou art the Imperishable Being, Not-Being, and That which transcends even these.

(38) Thou art the Primal God, the Ancient Being. Thou art the final resting place of this Universe. Thou art the Knower, the To-Be-Known, the Supreme Abode. By Thee, O myriad-formed, is the Universe pervaded.

(39) Thou art Vayu, Yama, Agni, Varuna, Shashanka, Prajapati and Prapitamaha. All hail to Thee, a thousand times all hail! Again and yet again, all hail to Thee!

(40) All hail to Thee from before and behind! All hail to Thee from every side, O All! Thy prowess is infinite, Thy might is measureless. Thou holdest all, therefore Thou art all.

There was once a woman in Madras who was a devotee of the Lord. She used to worship Him with her back towards the idol. A learned man rebuked her for doing so, but she cited this verse in reply, and the learned pundit was speechless. If all space is pervaded by God, when we find his eyes, ears and noses on all sides, why should we sit facing in a particular direction to worship Him?

(41) If ever in carelessness, thinking of Thee as comrade, I addressed Thee saying, "O Krishna! O Yadava!" not knowing Thy greatness in negligence or in affection;

(42) If ever I have been rude to Thee in jest, while at play, at rest-time, or at meals, while alone or in company, O Achyuta — forgive Thou my fault, I beg of Thee, O Incomprehensible One!

(43) Thou art Father of this world, of the moving and the unmoving. Thou art its adored, its worthiest Master. There is none equal to Thee. How then any greater than Thee? Thy power is matchless in the three worlds.

(44) Therefore, I prostrate myself before Thee, and beseech Thy grace, O Lord Adorable. As father with son, as comrade with comrade, so shouldst Thou bear, beloved Lord, with me, Thy loved one.

(45) I am filled with joy to see what never was seen before, and yet my heart is oppressed with fear. Show me that original form of Thine, O Lord. Be gracious, Devesha, O Jagannivasa!

(46) I crave to see Thee even as Thou wast, with crown, with mace, disc in hand. Wear Thou, once more, that four armed form, O thousand armed Yishvamurti!

The Lord said:

(47) It is to favor thee, O Arjuna, that I have revealed to thee, by My own unique power, this My Form — supreme, resplendent, universal, infinite, primal — which none save thee has ever seen.

(48) Not by the study of the Vedas, not by sacrifice, not by the study of other scriptures, not by gifts, nor yet by performance of rites or of fierce austerities can I, in such a form, be seen by anyone save thee in the world of men, O Kurupravira.

(49) Be thou neither oppressed nor bewildered to look on this awful form of Mine. Banish thy fear, ease thy mind, and lo! behold Me once again as I was.

Sanjaya said:

(50) So said Vasudeva to Arjuna, and revealed to him once more His original form. Wearing again His form benign, the *Mahatma* consoled him terrified.

Arjuna said:

(51) Beholding again Thy benign human form I am come to myself and am once more in my normal state.

The Lord said:

(52) Very hard to behold is that Form of Mine which thou hast seen. Even the gods always yearn to see it.

(53) Not by the Vedas, not by penance nor by gifts, nor yet by sacrifice can any behold Me in the Form that thou hast seen.

(54) But by single-minded devotion, O Arjuna, I may in this form be known and seen and truly entered into, O Parantapa.

First we should know the Lord, then see Him and then merge into Him. We may tell Him, "You may eat me up, I will not resist if You do. I am Yours, and I want to be one with You. What harm can it do even if You eat me up?" Telling us that He can grind us into paste with his teeth and throw it out, He tells us that we can know Him through *bhakti*. We can pass His test only through faith. When we know that everything takes place through Him and that we live and die as He wills, how can we be affected by anything?

(55) He alone comes to Me, O Pandava, who does My work, who has made Me his goal, who is My devotee, who has renounced attachment, and who has ill will towards none.

The Lord has given the whole substance of chapter eleven in this last verse. "He who works for Me, is ever devoted to Me, who is attached to nothing and bears ill will to none — not even to a person who may have committed a heinous sin — such a person comes to Me."

Chapter Twelve

Arjuna said:

(1) Of the devotees who thus worship Thee, incessantly attached, and those who worship the Imperishable Unmanifest, which are the better *yogis?*

The Lord said:

(2) Those I regard as the best *yogis* who, riveting their minds on Me, ever attached, worship Me with the highest faith.

(3) But those who worship the Imperishable, the Indefinable, the Unmanifest, the Omnipresent, the Unthinkable, the Rockseated, the Immovable, the Unchanging,

(4) Keeping the whole host of senses in complete control, looking on all with an impartial eye, engrossed in the welfare of all beings — these come indeed to Me.

(5) Greater is the travail of those whose mind is fixed on the Unmanifest; for it is hard for embodied mortals to gain the Unmanifest Goal.

Mortal man can only imagine the Unmanifest, the Impersonal, and as his language fails him he often negatively describes It as *"Neti, Neti."* ("Not that, not that.") Even iconoclasts are at bottom no better than idol-worshippers. To worship a book, to go to a church, or to pray with one's face in a particular direction — all these are forms of worshipping the Formless in an image or idol. And yet both the idol-breaker and the idol-worshipper cannot lose sight of the fact that there is something which is beyond all form — Unthinkable, Formless, Impersonal, Changeless.

The highest goal of the devotee is to become one with the object of his devotion. The *bhakta* extinguishes himself and merges into, becomes, God. This state can best be reached by devoting oneself to some form, and so it is said that the short cut to the Unmanifest is really the longest and the most difficult.

(6) But those who, casting all their actions on Me, making Me their all in all, worship Me with the meditation of undivided devotion —

(7) Of such, whose thoughts are centered on Me, O Partha, I become ere long the Deliverer from the ocean of this world of death.

These verses have given me great light. If a person feels that there is an Essence beyond this universe of objects with name and form and that he must know it, and if he leaves this world and withdraws into solitude with that aim, that is a legitimate path; but it is a difficult one even if one is sincere in one's aspiration to cultivate *bhakti* for the Unmanifest. The idea that the *Brahman* is real and that the visible universe is illusory is simply beyond the capacity of our reason to comprehend. How difficult it must be, then, to live according to it, to live forever absorbed in the *Atman*.

The path along which we have the least danger of falling into error is the one described in chapter two, beginning at verse 39. Neither Christians nor Muslims, nor certainly Hindus, have risen above the worship of the Personal God. Even a person who aspires to cultivate devotion exclusively for the Unmanifest worships some visible symbol. We can, of course, understand with our intellect the idea that the body is unconnected with the *Atman*; but has anyone ever been able to say what his state after death will be? The spiritualists and Theosophists are not correct, in my view, about what they say concerning spirits, in the sense that no one has been able to know and tell the whole truth.

For this reason, Shri Krishna told Arjuna that it would be better for him to take no interest in the problem at all. "Silence is golden in this matter," he says. "Don't you see, you dear simpleton, that I Myself have taken on a human body? And you ask Me, of all persons, whether worship of the Unmanifest is better, or that of the Personal God. You had better stop asking such questions and do as I tell you. Free yourself from all thoughts of violence and act towards all creatures with equal love and regard." If we understand this truth, we would escape many problems. We should not mind if, because we worship the Personal God, we are called idolaters and criticized for being so.

(8) On Me set thy mind, on Me rest thy conviction; thus without doubt shalt thou remain only in Me hereafter.

(9) If thou canst not set thy mind steadily on Me, then by the method of constant practice seek to win Me, O Dhananjaya.

What is the difference between constant practice and meditating on God? I think the former means listening to readings from holy books, reflecting on them and letting the mind dwell on their teachings. It means associating ourselves with men who are engaged in doing these things and listening to prayer songs and group devotions, for every little offering we make — leaf, flower, fruit or water — ultimately reaches God.

(10) If thou art also unequal to this method of constant practice, concentrate on service for Me, even thus serving Me thou shalt attain perfection.

(11) If thou art unable even to do this, then dedicating all to Me, with mind controlled, abandon the fruit of action.

(12) Better is knowledge than practice, better than knowledge is concentration, better than concentration is renunciation of the fruit of all action, from which directly issues peace.

Practice (*abhyasa*) is the practice of the *yoga* of meditation and control of psychic processes. Knowledge (*jnana*) is intellectual effort. Concentration (*dhyana*) is devoted worship. If as a result of all this there is no renunciation of the fruit of action, practice is no practice, knowledge is no knowledge, and concentration is no concentration.

(13) Who has ill will towards none, who is friendly and compassionate, who has shed all thought of "mine" or "I", who regards pain and pleasure alike, who is long-suffering,

[Upon hearing that one of the ashram boys had violently punished a dog:] Friendship can exist only between equals, but one should feel compassion towards all. We cannot throw a cricket bat at a dog to hit it. How would we feel if our parents or teachers did that to us? Even if we are obedient sons of our parents, how would we feel towards them if they threw a bat at us to hit us? We shall not discuss here what our duty towards a dog is. It is certain, however, that it is not right for us to hit one. Forgiveness lies in not being angry even with a dog which may have bitten us. "Tit for tat" is a wrong principle. It is certainly not based on forgiveness. What can we gain by being wicked with the wicked? The good lies only in our showing love and compassion even for such persons.

(14) Who is ever content, gifted with *yoga*, self-restrained, of firm conviction, who has dedicated his mind and reason to Me — that devotee (*bhakta*) of Mine is dear to Me.

(15) Who gives no trouble to the world, to whom the world causes no trouble, who is free from exultation, resentment, fear and vexation — that man is dear to Me.

(16) Who expects naught, who is pure, resourceful, unconcerned, untroubled, who indulges in no undertakings — that devotee of Mine is dear to Me.

The whole of chapter twelve describes the characteristics of a *bhakta*. If we compare it with chapter two, verses 55-72, which describe a man of steadfast wisdom [*sthitaprajna*], we shall find them similar.

"One who indulges in no undertakings" will not go in search of work. Work will come seeking him. God Himself will appoint his work and call him to it. Such a person, knowing that God shoulders the burdens of us all, leaves everything to Him. A slave need not go looking for work.

(17) Who rejoices not, neither frets nor grieves, who covets not, who abandons both good and ill — that devotee of Mine is dear to Me.

(18) Who is same to foe and friend, who regards alike respect and disrespect, cold and heat, pleasure and pain, who is free from attachment,

(19) Who weighs in equal scale blame and praise, who is silent, content with whatever his lot, who owns no home, who is of steady mind — that devotee of Mine is dear to Me.

"He does not get elated, though an emperor may bow to him," so sang Raychandbhai.

(20) They who follow this essence of *dharma* as I have told it, with faith, keeping Me as their goal — those devotees are exceedingly dear to Me.

All of us have our appointed tasks, as Brahmins or Kshatriyas, Vaisyas or Sudras [the four castes]. Anyone who does his work without hope of reward and in a disinterested spirit is a devotee of God. The second chapter contains verses describing a man of steadfast wisdom. They describe the state of mind of a *yogi* living absorbed in a mystic world. Chapter twelve describes, in our ordinary language, the state of mind of a *bhakta*.

Chapter Thirteen

From chapter thirteen begins a new subject. It discusses the body and its nature.

(1) This body, O Kaunteya, is called the Field. He who knows it is called the Knower of the Field by those who know.

Pandavas and Kauravas, that is, divine and demoniacal impulses, were fighting in this body, and God was watching the fight from a distance. Please do not believe that this is the history of a battle which took place on a little field near Hastinapur. The war is still going on. This is the verse we should keep in mind in order to understand the meaning of the phrase *dharmakshetra*, field of duty [in the Gita's first verse].

(2) And understand Me to be, O Bharata, the Knower of the Field in all the Fields; and the knowledge of the Field and the Knower of the Field, I hold, is true knowledge.

Our bodily life will have been lived to some purpose if it is spent in thinking which of these two [the Field or the Knower of the Field] we should serve and which we should go to for refuge.

(3) What that Field is, what its nature, what its modifications and whence, also who He [the Knower of the Field] is, and what His power — hear this briefly from Me.

---

(4) This subject has been sung by seers distinctly and in various ways, in different hymns as also in aphoristic texts about *Brahman,* well-reasoned and unequivocal.

This theme has been expounded analytically by seers in manifold ways in various hymns. It has been discussed in Vedanta texts with steps logically arranged and clearly explaining the connection between cause and effect; and every word has been weighed so that not a syllable could be altered.

(5) The great elements — Individuation, Reason, the Unmanifest, the ten senses and the one (mind), and the five spheres of the senses,

(6) Desire, dislike, pleasure, pain, association, consciousness, cohesion — this, in sum, is what is called the Field with its modifications.

"Association" means the power of the different elements in the body to cooperate with one another. "Cohesion" does not mean the abstract virtue of patience, but the property of the atoms in physical bodies to cohere.

(7) Freedom from pride and pretentiousness, nonviolence, forgiveness, uprightness, service of the Master, purity, steadfastness, self-restraint,

Outer and inner purity can be achieved by repeating *Ramanama* [God's name]. This purity can be properly preserved only if the heart is constantly kept clean by repeating *Ramanama.*

(8) Aversion from sense-objects, absence of conceit, realization of the painfulness and evil of birth, death, age and disease,

Aversion from objects of senses means the awareness that certain things ought to be treated as forbidden by us, that they ought to be unacceptable to us. The attributes described also include the realization of the evils of birth and death, of old age, disease and suffering. One who realizes this starts with the thought, "I am sin."

(9) Absence of attachment, refusal to be wrapped up in one's children, wife, home and family, even-mindedness whether good or ill befall,

(10) Unwavering and all-exclusive devotion to Me, resort to secluded spots, distaste for the haunts of men,

What does living in solitude mean? Retiring into a cave to live there alone by oneself? Our effort will have been worthwhile only if we can feel solitude even in the midst of a huge crowd.

(11) Settled conviction of the nature of the *Atman*, perception of the goal of the knowledge of Truth — all this is declared to be knowledge and the reverse of it is ignorance.

(12) I will (now) expound to thee that which is to be known and, knowing which, one enjoys immortality. It is the supreme *Brahman* which has no beginning, which is called neither Being nor Non-Being.

Why does Shri Krishna say this, when they say that the *Brahman* is *Sat-Chit-Ananda* [Being-Consciousness-Bliss] and that it alone is real? What he means to say is that *Brahman* does not mean Being, the contrary of Non-Being. When we use the word *Sat* in connection with the *Brahman*, its meaning transcends the two opposites and it signifies neither Being nor Non-Being. It is, so to say, a neutral term. God cannot be described as evil, nor as good. He is above either. The reality which is God is beyond the three categories of time.

(13) Everywhere having hands and feet, everywhere having eyes, heads, mouths, everywhere having ears, It abides embracing everything in the universe.

(14) Seeming to possess the functions of the senses, It is devoid of all the senses. It touches naught, upholds all. Having no *gunas*, It experiences *gunas*.

(15) Without all beings, yet within; immovable yet moving; so subtle that It cannot be perceived; so far and yet so near It is.

(16) Undivided, It seems to subsist divided in all beings. This *Brahman* — That which is to be known — is the Sustainer of all, yet It is their Devourer and Creator,

All contrary qualities are attributed to God because we cannot free our minds from dualities.

(17) Light of all lights, It is said to be beyond darkness. It is knowledge, the object of knowledge, to be gained only by knowledge. It is seated in the hearts of all.

He is the Superlight. He is beyond darkness. That is, He is Self-effulgent. He is Himself Knowledge. He is also the object of Knowledge to be realized only by Knowledge.

(18) Thus have I expounded in brief the Field, Knowledge and That which is to be known. My devotee, when he knows this, is worthy to become one with Me.

(19) Know that *prakriti* [nature] and *purusha* [soul] are both without beginning. Know that all the modifications and *gunas* [qualities of nature] are born of *prakriti*.

(20) *Prakriti* is described as the cause in the creation of effects from causes. *Purusha* is described as the cause of the experiencing of pleasure and pain.

God is described as having two aspects. Under one aspect we should know Him as *prakriti* and under the other as *purusha*. *Prakriti* is the cause of the creation of *karya*, anything done under compulsion of desires, and *karan*, the desires. *Purusha* is the cause of the experience of happiness and misery.

(21) For the *purusha*, residing in *prakriti*, experiences the *gunas* born of *prakriti*. Attachment to these *gunas* is the cause of his birth in good or evil wombs.

(22) What is called in this body the Witness, the Assentor, the Sustainer, the Experiencer, the Great Lord and also the Supreme *Atman*, is the Supreme Being.

The *purusha* dwelling in this body is *para*, that is, "beyond" *prakriti*, but He witnesses and gives consent. He sustains everything, and is also the Enjoyer. He is moreover, the God of gods and is described as *Paramatnan.*

(23) He who thus knows *purusha* and *prakriti* with its *gunas* is not born again, no matter how he live and move.

This verse does not sanction self-indulgence, but points out the great value of *bhakti.*

Every *karma* has the effect of binding the soul, but one can become free from the bonds of *karma* by dedicating all one's *karma* to God. Thus, anyone who has become free from the egotistic idea of being the author of anything, and who recognizes every moment of his life the authority of the Dweller within, will never commit sin. It is in egotism that sin has its source. There is no sin where there is no consciousness of the "I".

If anyone claims that he is a *bhakta* of God and that, therefore, the sins he may commit are committed by God, he is wrong.. On the other hand it would be right if the world were to say of him that he was a man of God and that everything he did was done through him by God.

If anyone asks us whether we have attained spiritual knowledge, our reply should be, "Only God knows. I do not know." Our reason may be carried away by pride at any time and become evil, but the man who has attained to perfect knowledge will never be misguided by his reason.

(24) Some through meditation behold the *Atman* by themselves in their own self, others by *Sankhya yoga,* and others by *karma yoga.*

(25) Yet others, not knowing (Him) thus, worship (Him) having heard from others. They too pass beyond death, because of devoted adherence to what they heard.

(26) Wherever something is born, animate or inanimate, know, thou Bharatarshabha, that it issues from the union of the Field and the Knower of the Field.

If we examine things separately — human beings, grains of dust, water, and so on — our conclusions about their origin will be different in each case. If, instead, we go to the very first cause, we shall no more think of objects having their distinctive forms and names.

(27) Who sees abiding in all beings the same Parameshvara [Supreme Lord], imperishable in the perishable, he sees indeed.

Though things are ever perishing, there is an indestructible element in everything which remains unaffected by any change. He alone sees who sees this.

(28) When he sees the same Ishvara [Lord] abiding everywhere alike, he does not hurt Himself by himself and hence he attains the highest goal.

When he sees the same God abiding alike at all places he does not destroy the Self [*Atman*] by the self. He believes that, with the destruction of his body, he himself does not perish, and consequently he achieves the highest status.

(29) Who sees that it is *prakriti* that performs all actions and thus (knows) that *Atman* performs them not, he sees indeed.

(30) When he sees the diversity of Being as founded in unity and the whole expanse issuing therefrom, then he attains to *Brahman*.

(31) This Imperishable, Supreme *Atman*, O Kaunteya, though residing in the body, acts not and is not stained, for He has no beginning and no *gunas*.

(32) As the all-pervading ether, by reason of its subtlety, is not soiled, even so *Atman* pervading every part of the body is not soiled.

(33) As the one Sun illumines the whole universe, even so the Master of the Field illumines the whole field.

(34) Those who, with the eyes of knowledge, thus perceive the distinction between the Field and the Knower of the Field, and (the secret) of the release of beings from *prakriti*, they attain to the Supreme.

In chapter thirteen Shri Krishna has explained the nature of the Field and the Knower of the Field, the means of understanding the nature of each and the different characteristics of such knowledge. However great one's knowledge, if one is proud of that knowledge, one has read the Gita in vain. Where there is pride, there is no knowledge.

A man who has knowledge is always free from pride and ostentation, is straightforward, serves his guru, is pure and steady, is a man of self-control, and is free from egotism. He does not suffer because of old age and disease. He is not attached to his son or wife or home, is filled with unswerving devotion for the Lord, lives in solitude, takes interest in spiritual studies and is devoted to the pursuit of philosophic truth.

Chapter Fourteen

We assemble here for studying the Gita, that is, for learning to follow its teaching in daily life. When we have a stomach ache, we consult a book of home remedies and use the medicine suggested. The Gita is such a book of home remedies for us. We should make it our only source as far as possible. We may consult any number of books in the world in support of what we derive from the Gita, but should be satisfied with its sole authority. For this, we should have single-minded devotion to it. Such devotion should become spontaneous in us.

In a certain place, people used secretly to catch fish from the village pond. The village committee decided, since in any case people caught fish — did so in secret and were then afraid of being discovered — that they should be required to take out licenses for catching fish and some revenue raised by that means. This led to a dispute between two parties and the dispute was brought to me for settlement. I was afraid to give a decision, for people are not content to leave it to others to exercise discrimination in religious matters and faith on their behalf.

If we are guided by some other person's ideas about *dharma*, we would be lost when he was dead. It would have been much better if those village people had decided to consult the Gita or the Veda or the Koran, instead of asking me. We should look upon any of these works as the means of solving our spiritual problems; but I was told in reply to this suggestion that one could find support from a book for any idea.

When the authors of the *shastras* said that Sudras and others should not read Vedas and other sacred works, probably their reason was that the latter might interpret these works to justify their own wishes in particular matters. Anyone who approaches the *shastras* without scrupulous regard for Truth and nonviolence will derive no benefit from them. It is possible to draw any number of evil ideas from the Bible, the Vedas, the Koran and other scriptures. I have come across persons who justified even murder on the authority of these works.

The Gita, however, will serve as a safe guide to anyone who reads it with Truth and nonviolence as his guiding principles. Everyone should decide for himself with its help. Instead of borrowing faith from others, one should have one's own faith and come to decisions accordingly. If the intention is sincere and there is no desire for outward show, any error that the decision may contain will be forgiven. A person acting in this manner learns a lesson from his error and discovers the right path.

(1) Yet again will I expound the highest and the best of all knowledge, knowing which all the sages passed hence to the highest perfection.

(2) By having recourse to this knowledge they became one with Me. They need not come to birth even at a creation, nor do they suffer at a dissolution.

(3) The great *prakriti* is for me the womb in which I deposit the germ. From it all beings come to birth, O Bharata.

Among the very first sentences in the Bible is, "God said let there be light, and there was light." That is, let there be a universe, and a universe came into existence. A potter has to mold clay into a shape on his wheel and then put the thing into fire to bake. God does not have to act in that manner. He is a magician, He simply puts the seed in his imagination — which is *prakriti*, Lakshmi or Mother Goddess of the world — and the universe comes into existence.

(4) Whatever forms take birth in the various species, the great *prakriti* is their Mother, and I the seed-giving Father.

(5) *Sattva, rajas* and *tamas* are the *gunas* [qualities] sprung from *prakriti*. It is they, O Mahabahu, that keep the imperishable Dweller bound to the body.

(6) Of these, *sattva*, being stainless, is light-giving and healing. It binds with the bond of happiness and the bond of knowledge, O sinless one.

Those persons whose food, recreation and thoughts are *sattvic* are healthy. A person who merely eats *sattvic* food but is not *sattvic* in his general way of living and in his thoughts should be looked upon as diseased person.

(7) *Rajas*, know thou, is of the nature of passion, the source of thirst and attachment. It keeps man bound with the bond of action.

Know that *rajas* is associated with desire. This may mean either that it has its source in, or that it is the cause of, desire. It creates attachment for cravings. It keeps the embodied one (i.e. the living being) bound with the bond of *karma*.

(8) *Tamas*, know thou, is born of ignorance, of mortal man's delusion. It keeps him bound with heedlessness, sloth and slumber, O Bharata.

Pramad [heedlessness] means all kinds of unworthy wishes arising in us. *Alas* [sloth] is *pramad* in a worse form still. *Nidra* [slumber], which is next, is the state of mind natural to those sunk in darkness. A man who is established in *samadhi* and is always awake feels no need to recline for rest or stretch his limbs for relaxation.

(9) *Sattva* attaches man to happiness, *rajas* to action, and *tamas*, shrouding knowledge, attaches him to heedlessness.

Sattva leads to happiness and the quality of *rajas* to *karma*. (This is not *karma* as it is defined in the Gita. It is the *karma* of him who is always doing something or other without pausing to think.) *Tamas* covers up knowledge and leads to heedlessness.

(10) *Sattva* prevails, O Bharata, having overcome *rajas* and *tamas*; *rajas*, when it has overpowered *sattva* and *tamas*; likewise *tamas* reigns when *sattva* and *rajas* are crushed.

If a person overcomes *rajas* and *tamas*, he can create *sattva*. All the three exist in us. We should make a special effort to cultivate that which we want to strengthen.

(11) When the light — knowledge — shines forth from all the gates of this body, then it may be known that the *sattva* thrives.

(12) Greed, activity, assumption of undertakings, restlessness, craving — these are in evidence when *rajas* flourishes, O Bharatarshabha.

(13) Ignorance, dullness, heedlessness and delusion — these are in evidence when *tamas* reigns, O Kurunandana.

(14) If the embodied one meets his end whilst *sattva* prevails, then he attains to the spotless worlds of the knowers of the Highest.

That is, he attains spiritual welfare. When he is nearing death, such a person refuses to take any medicine which may be offered, and says that he will have nothing but Ganges water. He who awaits death in peace in this manner is a *sattvic* man.

(15) If he dies during the reign within him of *rajas*, he is born among men attached to action. And if he dies in *tamas*, he is born in a species not endowed with reason.

(16) The fruit of *sattvic* action is said to be stainless merit; that of *rajas* is pain, and that of *tamas* ignorance.

(17) Of *sattva*, knowledge is born; of rajas, greed; of *tamas*, heedlessness, delusion and ignorance.

(18) Those abiding in *sattva* rise upwards, those in *rajas* stay midway, those in *tamas* sink downwards.

(19) When the seer perceives no agent another than the *gunas* and knows Him who is above the *gunas*, he attains to My being.

As soon as a man realizes that he is not the doer, but the *gunas* are the agent, the self vanishes, and he goes through all his actions spontaneously, just to sustain the body. And as the body is meant to observe the highest end, all his actions will ever reveal detachment and dispassion. Such a seer can easily have a glimpse of the One who is above the *gunas* and offer his devotion to Him.

(20) When the *Atman* dwelling as witness in this body sees none else, but knows only Him who is above the *gunas*, that person comes to Me.

Arjuna said:

(21) What, O Lord, are the marks of him who has transcended the three *gunas*? How does he conduct himself? How does he transcend the three *gunas*?

The Lord said:

(22) He, O Pandava, who does not disdain light, activity, and delusion when they come into being, nor desires them when they vanish;

The Lord replies, "He who transcends the three *gunas* does not suffer because of light or activity or darkness — that is, when any of them predominates over the others — and does not wish that it should prevail or subside."

This is one of the few difficult verses in the Gita. Should not one wish to have knowledge? In fact, in the best Vedic prayer, the Gayatri Mantra, we pray to the shining Being to purify our intellect, to make it *sattvic*. We also pray, "Take me from darkness to light." We aspire to be lifted from the darkness of attachment to illumination. If we, living in the ashram, did not cherish this aspiration, we would fail in our aims.

What, then, should we make of the statement in this verse? That we should not mind even if the slumber becomes deeper, should not even wish to get out of it? Should we say, "I have no wish, the three states are the same to me?" If anyone feels thus, you may be sure he will be totally ruined. Either we should regard this verse as an interpolation, or as the very key to the meaning of the Gita.

If you remember, in the beginning Arjuna does not ask whether or not it is proper to kill, but asks what good he could expect from killing his kinsmen. And so the Lord asks him, "What is this distinction you make between kinsmen and others? Your duty is to do the job of killing, irrespective of whether they are your kinsmen or others." Similarly, Arjuna does not here ask Shri Krishna which of the three *gunas* is best. He knows that ultimately one must transcend all the three. We can know a person who possesses one of the three *gunas*. It is not difficult to distinguish among the three classes. "But," he asks, "can we find anyone in this world who has risen above the *gunas* altogether?" This verse gives the Lord's reply to that question.

What other reply could He give? A person who has risen above the three *gunas* will not let himself be deceived by the threefold distinction of good, bad and indifferent, and we shall not see in him the effects of any of the three *gunas*. He will not seem to the world to be happy when one sees activity or unhappy when one sees lethargy. Such a person has come out of the duality of happiness and misery. He has risen above the pairs of opposites. A person like this should seem to us untouched, unconcerned, by anything. He should be absolutely free from egotism.

The Bhagavad Gita has stressed this point again and again. It teaches you just one thing, to shed the thought of "I" in such matters. A person who has risen above the three *gunas* should appear to the world to be a cipher, a mere stone. That is, he should have got rid of his "I".

But when can one be in such a state? Shri Rajchandra sings, "When the body has become as the burnt rope." That should be our condition. When a rope is burnt, only its form remains, and none of its other properties survive. Such a rope may be said to have risen above the three *gunas*, for it no longer has the property in virtue of which it can be used for connecting or binding things or drawing water from a well.

A person who has risen above the three *gunas* is like such a rope. As a rope may produce on us the illusion of a snake, so we may think of such a person as being like inert stone or having no interest in any activity, but he does not care. It is our *dharma* to be like such burnt rope.

The only way, then, of rising to this state beyond the three *gunas* is to cultivate the *sattvic* quality; for in order to rise to that state one is required to cultivate the virtues of fearlessness, humility, sincerity, and so on. So long as we live in the body, there is some evil, some violence. The most, therefore, that we can do is to be *sattvic* in the highest degree possible. That is why we pray, "Take me from darkness to light."

(23) He who, seated as one indifferent, is not shaken by the *gunas* and stays still and moves not, knowing it is the *gunas* playing their parts,

(24) He who holds pleasure and pain alike, who is sedate,

who regards earth, stone and gold as all the same, who is wise, and weighs in equal scale things pleasant and unpleasant, who is even-minded in praise and blame,

(25) Who holds alike respect and disrespect, who is the same to friend and foe, who indulges in no undertaking — that man is called *gunatita* [beyond the *gunas*].

We who are every moment of our lives acting as though we were the doers can only imagine this state. We can hardly experience it; but we can hitch our wagon to that star and work our way closer and closer towards it by gradually withdrawing the self from our actions.

A *gunatita* has experience of his own condition but he cannot describe it, for he who can describe it ceases to be one. The moment he proceeds to do so, self peeps in.

(26) He who serves Me with an unwavering and exclusive *bhakti yoga* transcends these *gunas* and is worthy to become one with *Brahman*.

(27) For I am the very image of *Brahman*, changeless and deathless, as also of everlasting *dharma* and perfect bliss.

A person who struggles ceaselessly and hard to overcome his shortcomings may not perhaps succeed in this birth in overcoming them all, but, in the end he will surely benefit. Today the world will censure him for his "shortcomings." If, however, he bears all that in patience and strives ever harder, he is sure, ultimately, to get peace of mind. Peace lies in the very fact of struggling. It is a source of great reassurance. Hence, we should strive to cultivate *sattvic* qualities.

Chapter Fifteen

The Lord said:

(1) With its root above and branches below, the ashvattha tree, they say, is imperishable. It has Vedic hymns for leaves. He who knows it knows the Vedas.

Shvah means tomorrow, and *ashvattha* (*na shvopi shthata*) means that which will not last even until tomorrow, i.e., the world of sense which is every moment in a state of flux; but even though it is perpetually changing, at its root is *Brahman* or the Supreme. It is imperishable. It has for its protection and support the leaves of the Vedic hymns, i.e., *dharma*. He who knows the world of sense as such [perpetually changing yet imperishable at its roots], and who knows *dharma*, is the real man of wisdom. That man has really known the Vedas.

(2) Above and below its branches spread, blossoming because of the *gunas*, having for their shoots the sense-objects. Deep down in the world of men are ramified its roots in the shape of the consequences of action.

This is the description of the tree of the world of sense as the unenlightened see it. They fail to discover its root above in the *Brahman* and so they are always attached to the objects of sense. They water the tree with the three *gunas* and remain bound to *karma* in the world of men.

---

(3) Its true form is not here perceived, neither is its end, nor beginning, nor basis. Let men first hew down this deep-rooted *ashvattha* with the sure weapon of detachment.

(4) Let him pray to win that haven from which there is no return and seek to find refuge in the Primal Being from whom has emanated this ancient world of action.

We shall remain apart from this world, while working in it, when we regard it as the sphere in which people run after enjoyments, and cut it off at the root with the weapon of non-cooperation. In no other way is it possible to cut it off at the roots, for it is without beginning and without end. That is why Shri Krishna has advised noncooperation.

(5) To that imperishable haven those enlightened souls go who are without pride and delusion, who have triumphed over the taints of attachment, who are ever in tune with the Supreme, whose passions have died, and who are exempt from the pairs of opposites such as pleasure and pain.

(6) Neither the sun, nor the moon, nor fire illumine it. Men who arrive there return not — that is My supreme abode.

(7) A part indeed of Myself which has been the eternal *jiva* [the individual soul] in this world of life attracts the mind and the five senses from their place in *prakriti*.

(8) When the Master (of the body) acquires a body and discards it, He carries these with Him wherever He goes, even as the wind carries scents from flower-beds.

(9) Having settled Himself in the senses — ear, eye, touch taste, and smell, as well as the mind — through them He frequents their objects.

(10) The deluded perceive Him not as He leaves or settles in (a body) or enjoys (sense-objects) in association with the *gunas*. It is only those endowed with the eye of knowledge that see Him.

We see only the world, but do not see God who is immanent in it.

(11) *Yogis* who strive see Him seated in themselves. The witless ones who have not cleaned themselves see Him not, even though they strive.

This does not conflict with the covenant that God has made even with the sinner in chapter nine, verse 30. *Akritatman* (he who has not cleansed himself) means one who has no devotion in him, who has not made up his mind to purify himself.

The most confirmed sinner, if he has humility enough to seek refuge in surrender to God, purifies himself and succeeds in finding Him. Those who do not care to observe the cardinal and the casual vows [*yama-niyama*] and expect to find God through bare intellectual exercise are witless, godless. They will not find Him.

(12) The light in the sun which illumines the whole universe, and which is in the moon and in the fire — that light, know thou, is mine.

(13) It is I who, penetrating the earth, uphold all beings with my strength, and becoming the moon — the essence of all sap — nourish all herbs.

(14) It is I who, becoming the Vaishvanara Fire and entering the bodies of all that breathe, assimilate the four kinds of food with the help of the outward and the inward breaths.

Vaishvanara means the heat which digests food. The four types of food are: what is sucked, what is licked, what is drunk and what is eaten.

(15) And I am seated in the hearts of all. From Me proceed memory, knowledge and the intellect. It is I who am to be known in all the Vedas; I, the author of Vedanta and the knower of the Vedas.

(16) There are two Beings in the world: *kshara* (perishable) and *akshara* (imperishable). *Kshara* embraces all creatures and their permanent basis is *akshara*.

(17) The Supreme Being is surely another — called *Paramatman* — who as the Imperishable Ishvara pervades and supports the three worlds.

(18) Because I transcend the *kshara* and am also higher than the *akshara*, I am known in the world and in the Vedas as Purushottama (the Highest Being).

(19) He who, undeluded, knows Me as Purushottama, knows all. He worships Me with all his heart, O Bharata.

He is above all opposites. Once we have risen above this world, which is but *maya* [illusion], need we think of God as its author?

(20) Thus I have revealed to thee, sinless one, this most mysterious *shastra*. He who understands this, O Bharata, is a man of understanding. He has fulfilled his life's mission.

"I have disclosed to thee this most secret (the best even of the best) *shastra*. He who understands this becomes a man of understanding, fulfills his life's mission, and also becomes free from his debt."

Chapter Sixteen

The Lord said:

(1) Fearlessness, purity of heart, steadfastness in *jnana* and *yoga* — knowledge and action — beneficence, self-restraint, sacrifice, spiritual study, austerity and uprightness,

(2) Nonviolence, truth, slowness to wrath, the spirit of dedication, serenity, aversion to slander, tenderness to all that lives, freedom from greed, gentleness, modesty, freedom from levity,

(3) Spiritedness, forgiveness, fortitude, purity, freedom from ill will and arrogance — these are to be found in one born with the divine heritage, O Bharata.

(4) Pretentiousness, arrogance, self-conceit, wrath, coarseness, ignorance — these are to be found in one born with the devilish heritage.

(5) The divine heritage makes for freedom; the devilish, for bondage. Grieve not. O Partha. Thou art born with a divine heritage.

(6) There are two orders of created beings in the world — the divine and the devilish. The divine order has been described in detail, hear from Me now of the devilish, O Partha.

(7) Men of the devil do not know what they may do and what they may not. Neither purity, nor right conduct, nor truth is to be found in them.

Those who lack purity and truthfulness and whose conduct is not moral are diseased men and women. There can be no
disease unless there is mental evil or bodily error. A person whose
Atman is awake every moment of his life constantly prays that
his body be filled with light. How did Ladha Maharaj overcome
his *leukoderma* [skin disease]? Every time he applied the bel leaves
on the affected parts, he prayed that light should enter his body.

We can prevent unhealthy emotions from disturbing our
body only if we daily pray for the flow of light into it. I would
ask every person who suffers from a disease if he is free from
attachments and aversions. Outwardly we may be clean and our
conduct may be moral, but, in the absence of truthfulness, it is
all as hollow as a drum. We gather here to cultivate that truthfulness.

(8) "Without truth, without basis, without God is the
universe," they say. "Born of the union of the sexes,
prompted by naught but lust."

(9) Holding this view, these depraved souls of feeble understanding and of fierce deeds come forth as enemies of
the world to destroy it.

(10) Given to insatiable lust, possessed by pretentiousness, arrogance and conceit, they seize wicked purpose in
their delusion and go about with sinful bent of mind.

(11) Given to boundless cares that end only with their
death, making indulgence or lust their sole goal, convinced
that that is all,

(12) Caught in myriad snares of hope, slaves to lust and
wrath, they seek unlawfully to amass wealth for the satisfaction of their appetites.

Anger consumes many times more energy than does joy. It is because people spend more energy than they can afford that injustice and tyranny prevail in the world. Enjoyment of sense-pleasure leads to death. If people gave themselves up to it, God's rule in the world would end and Satan's prevail. *Brahmacharya* leads to immortality.

(13) "This have I gained today. This aspiration shall I now attain. This wealth is mine. This likewise shall be mine hereafter."

(14) "This enemy I have already slain. Others also I shall slay. Lord of all am I. Enjoyment is mine. Perfection is mine. Strength is mine. Happiness is mine."

(15) "Wealthy am I and high-born. What other is like unto me? I shall perform a sacrifice. I shall give alms. I shall be merry!" Thus think they, by ignorance deluded;

Living in this way, man gambles away the *ratnachintamani* [a precious stone which yields everything that is desired] of his body. We must strive our best to raise ourselves to a higher level.

(16) And tossed about by diverse fancies, caught in the net of delusion, stuck deep in the indulgence of appetites, into foul hell they fall.

(17) Wise in their own conceit, stubborn, full of the intoxication of pelf and pride, they offer nominal sacrifices for show, contrary to the rule.

(18) Given to pride, force, arrogance, lust and wrath they are deriders indeed, scorning Me in their own and others' bodies.

(19) These cruel scorners, lowest of mankind and vile, I hurl down again into devilish wombs.

(20) Doomed to devilish wombs, these deluded ones, far from ever coming to Me, sink lower and lower in birth after birth.

(21) Threefold is this gate of hell leading man to perdition — lust, wrath and greed. These three, therefore, should be shunned.

One who keeps himself free from these does not devote himself to the pursuit of worldly happiness, but follows the path of spiritual welfare.

(22) The man who escapes these three gates of darkness, O Kaunteya, works out his welfare and thence reaches the highest state.

(23) He who forsakes the rule of *shastra* and does but the bidding of his selfish desires gains neither perfection, nor happiness, nor the highest state.

The literal meaning of the verse is that so long as one's intellect has not become vigilant and the heart is not filled exclusively with *Ramanama*, one should be ruled by the authority of the *shastras* — the Vedas, the works of history, the Puranas. They, however, contain contradictory statements. If our foundations are not strong, consulting a *shastra* will avail us nothing.

The derived meaning is that we should be guided by *shishtachara* [the prevailing standard of right conduct], that is, we should follow the example of those forefathers of ours who were holy and fearless. *Shishtachara* may be disregarded only if it requires one to violate Truth.

(24) Therefore let *shastra* be thy authority for determining what ought to be done and what ought not to be done. Ascertain thou the rule of the *shastra* and do thy task here (accordingly).

The intention in this verse is to tell us not to look upon ourselves as an authority, that is, not to be guided by our wishes and feelings. So long as one's intellect has not become vigilant and the heart is not filled exclusively with *Ramanama*, one should be ruled by the authority of *shastra*. *Shastra* here has the same meaning as in the preceding verse: the path of self-restraint laid down by the seers and saints.

Chapter Seventeen

Arjuna said:

(1) What, then, O Krishna, is the position of those who forsake the rule of *shastra* and yet worship with faith? Do they act from *sattva* or *rajas* or *tamas*?

"Forsake the rule of shastra" means disregard the *shishtachara* [conduct of the worthy], or without the guidance of a guru. "With faith" means with some little humility. Shri Krishna's reply to this is indirect. Not to accept *shastra* as an authority and to have faith are inconsistent with each other. Faith consists in accepting the authority of *shastra*.

Shri Krishna replies:

(2) Threefold is the faith of men — an expression of their nature in each case. It is *sattvic, rajasic* or *tamasic.* Hear thou of it.

Shri Krishna thinks that He might humor Arjuna a little. He assumes that a person may disregard the *shastras.*

(3) The faith of every man is in accord with his innate character. Man is made up of faith. Whatever his object of faith, even so is he.

(4) *Sattvic* persons worship the gods; *rajasic* ones the *yakshas* [demigods] and *rakshasas* [demons]; and others — men of *tamas* — worship *manes* and spirits.

It is said that one cannot get knowledge without a guru. The moment you have found one, you know what the *shishtachara* is. But these are such hard times that one does not easily find a guru. If we are doing God's work, it is bound to be in harmony with *shishtachara*. That is why we are enjoined to keep repeating the Lord's name while doing any work. This verse explains in what spirit we should do this. Our faith must not be in ghosts and spirits or in demons. We ought to pray only to a beneficent deity.

(5) Those men who, wedded to pretentiousness and arrogance, possessed by the violence of lust and passion, practice fierce austerity not ordained by *shastra* —

(6) They, while they torture the several elements that make up their bodies, torture Me too dwelling in them. Know them to be of unholy resolves.

Any *shastra* which seeks to suppress Truth is of little use. Those who follow such a *shastra* are men of demoniac inclination. If Truth is timeless, so is untruth, and, likewise, if light is timeless, so is darkness, too. We should embrace what is timeless only if it is combined with Truth.

(7) Of three kinds again is the food that is dear to each; so also are sacrifice, austerity, and charity. Hear how they differ.

(8) Victuals that add to one's years vitality, strength, health, happiness and appetite, and are savory, rich, substantial and inviting are dear to the *sattvic*.

(9) Victuals that are bitter, sour, salty, overhot, spicy, dry, burning, and causing pain, bitterness and disease are dear to the *rajas*.

(10) Food which has become cold, insipid, putrid, stale, discarded and unfit for sacrifice, is dear to the *tamas*.

If we cling to this classification, we shall not come to the right conclusion. Lovers of *ladua* [a popular sweet] have included *ladus* in *sattvic* food. Ladus do not help one to safeguard one's *Brahmacharya*. In interpreting the meaning of "inviting", too, we should use discrimination. There must have been a reason in that age for making such a classification. There must have been persons even then who would eat a handful of chiles at a time.

In the present age, there is no need for eating foods containing fat. If here we start eating *ghee* [clarified butter], our food will be not *sattvic* or *rajasic*, but such as a demon would love. The inclusion of bitter, sour and saltish foods is quite correct. Then the verse mentions food which has been left over. Stilton cheese (a food containing countless germs) is of this class. Processed grain and rice do not belong to this class.

(11) That sacrifice is *sattvic* which is willingly offered as a duty, without desire for fruit and according to the rule.

(12) But when sacrifice is offered with an eye to fruit and for vainglory, know, O Bharatashreshtha, that it is *rajas*.

(13) Sacrifice which is contrary to the rule, which produces no food, which lacks the sacred text, which involves no giving up and which is devoid of faith is said to be *tamas*.

"No giving up," means one in which no gifts are made to the poor.

(14) Homage to the gods, to Brahmins, to *gurus* and to wise men; cleanliness, uprightness, *Brahmacharya* and non-violence — these constitute austerity (*tapas*) of the body.

(15) Words that cause no hurt, that are true, loving and helpful, and spiritual study, constitute austerity of speech.

(16) Serenity, benignity, silence, self-restraint, and purity of the spirit — these constitute austerity of the mind.

(17) This threefold austerity practiced in perfect faith by men not desirous of fruit, disciplined, is said to be *sattvic*.

(18) Austerity which is practiced with an eye to gain praise, honor and homage, and for ostentation, is said to be *rajas*. It is fleeting and unstable.

(19) Austerity which is practiced from any foolish obsession, either to torture oneself or to procure another's ruin, is called *tamas*.

A person who fasts for a hundred days or keeps standing on one foot performs not *sattvic* but *tamasic tapas*.

(20) Charity given as a matter of duty to one who is not in a position to do good in turn, at the right place and time, and to the right person, is said to be *sattvic*.

It may not, in all circumstances, be right to give what it is right to give in certain circumstances. This is also true about recipients. It is but right to give food to one who has lost the use of his limbs altogether; but suppose there is a blind man who is suffering from fever and comes begging. He would be an unworthy object of our charity if we gave him food. If we give him a blanket and he sells it, then also will our gift have been made to an unworthy person. In one place, it may be right to give food, in another something else, and in still another a third thing. The principle is the same in all cases, but its application will vary according to place, time and person.

(21) Charity which is given either in the hope of receiving in return, or with a view to winning merit, or grudgingly, is declared to be *rajas*.

(22) Charity given at the wrong place and time, and to an undeserving recipient, disrespectfully and with contempt, is declared to be *tamas*.

(23) *Aum-Tat-Sat* has been declared to be the threefold name of *Brahman* and by that name were created of old the *Brahmanas*, the Vedas and sacrifices.

[*"Aum-Tat-Sat* is one composite formula of dedication to God. *Aum* is an expression of the Being subsisting everywhere in all times; *Tat* expresses the Supreme in its detachment; and *Sat* expresses Truth and Goodness and Beauty." — Desai, p. 361]

(24) Therefore, with *Aum* ever on their lips, all the rites of sacrifice, charity and austerity proceed always according to the rule by Brahmavadins [devotees of *Brahman*].

(25) With utterance of *Tat* and without desire for fruit are the several rites of sacrifice, austerity and charity performed by those seeking freedom.

(26) *Sat* is employed in the, sense of "real" and "good", O Partha. *Sat* is also applied to beautiful deeds.

(27) Constancy in sacrifice, austerity and charity is called *Sat*, and all work for these purposes is also *Sat*.

The substance of the last four *shlokas* is that every action should be done in a spirit of complete dedication to God, for *Aum* alone is the only reality. That only which is dedicated to It counts.

(28) Whatever is done, O Partha, by way of sacrifice — charity or austerity or any other work — is called *Asat* if done without faith. It counts for naught hereafter, as here.

Aum-Tat-Sat means that all that exists is *Aum*, that our "I" is unreal, that God alone is and nothing else is real, that we are all running after things in vain.

We should resolve that we wish to live as ciphers in this world. The world may kick us from one place to another as if we were a ball, but we will not let ourselves be so kicked. We will use our knowledge, our bodies, our strength and money, all for the service of others, and that, too, not with the desire to earn a good name for ourselves. Thus, *Aum-Tat-Sat* is a vow of humility. It teaches us to realize our utter insignificance, to be completely free from egotism.

The threefold classification of gifts, faith, austerities, etc., given in this chapter is only an illustration. We can make as many categories as we like. The intention here was to show that the reign of the three *gunas* prevails throughout the universe. Existing apart from the three *gunas* is God. We have to merge in Him. Even if we cultivate the *sattvic* qualities to their highest perfection in us, something of *rajasic* and *tamasic* will remain. But, without worrying ourselves about this, we should continue to strive and cultivate finer and finer *sattvic* qualities in us; for the impulses which agitate us the least and consume the least amount of our energy are *sattvic* impulses.

Chapter Eighteen

Arjuna said:

(1) Mahabahu! I would fain learn severally the secret of *sannyasa* and of *tyaga*, O Hrishikesha, O Keshinshudana.

The Lord replies:

(2) Renunciation of actions springing from selfish desire is described as *sannyasa* by the seers. Abandonment of the fruit of all action is called *tyaga* by the wise.

(3) Some thoughtful persons say, "All action should be abandoned as an evil." Others say, "Action for sacrifice, charity and austerity should not be relinquished."

(4) Hear my decision in this matter of *tyaga*, O Bharatasattama; for *tyaga*, too, O mightiest of men, has been described to be of three kinds.

(5) Action for sacrifice, charity and austerity may not be abandoned. It must needs be performed. Sacrifice, charity and austerity are purifiers of the wise.

(6) But even these actions should be performed abandoning all attachment and fruit. Such, O Partha, is my best and considered opinion.

(7) It is not right to renounce one's allotted task. Its abandonment, from delusion, is said to be *tamas*.

(8) He who abandons action, deeming it painful and for fear of straining his limbs — he will never gain the fruit of abandonment for his abandonment is *rajas*.

(9) But when an allotted task is performed from a sense of duty and with abandonment of attachments and fruit, O Arjuna, that abandonment is deemed to be *sattvic*.

(10) Neither does he disdain unpleasant action, nor does he cling to pleasant action — this wise man full of *sattva*, who practices abandonment, and who has shaken off all doubts.

(11) For the embodied one cannot completely abandon action; but he who abandons the fruit of action is named a *tyagi*.

By the *sannyasa* mentioned in the first verse, the poet meant renunciation of all *karmas*; but total renunciation of *karma* is impossible while we live in the body and the *Atman's* connection with the body will remain right till the moment of death. All that we can do therefore, is to shun *karmas* which have any trace of egotism in them and engage ourselves only in *karma* which is in the nature of a duty for us. One should work without selfish motives. The state of mind in which such motives will have disappeared most is the *sattvic* state.

(12) To those who do not practice abandonment accrues, when they pass away, the fruit of action which is of three kinds — disagreeable, agreeable, mixed — but never to the *sannyasis*.

(13) Learn, from me, O Mahabahu, the five factors mentioned in the *Sankhya* doctrine for the accomplishment of all action:

(14) The field, the doer, the various means, the several different operations, fifth and the last, the Unseen.

(15) Whatever action, right or wrong, a man undertakes to do with the body, speech or mind, these are the five factors thereof.

(16) This being so, he who, by reason of unenlightened intellect, sees the unconditioned *Atman* as the agent — such a man is dense and unseeing.

(17) He who is free from all sense of "I", whose motive is untainted, slays not nor is bound, even though he slay these worlds.

If read superficially, this verse is likely to mislead the reader. We shall not find anywhere in the world a perfect example of such a person. As in geometry we require imaginary, ideal figures, so in practical affairs, too, we require ideal instances when discussing ethical issues. This verse, therefore, can be construed thus only: "We may say (for the sake of argument) that he whose sense of 'I' has melted away altogether and whose reason is tainted with no trace of evil whatever can kill the entire world; but one who is completely free from the egotistic sense of 'I' has no body, and one whose reason is absolutely pure is simultaneously conscious of time in all its categories, past, present and future, and there is only one such being — God — Who does nothing though doing everything and Who is nonviolent though He kills." Man therefore, has only one course open to him, that of not killing and of following the *shishtachara* — of following *shastra*.

(18) Knowledge, the object of knowledge, and the knower compose the threefold urge to action. The means, the action and the doer compose the threefold sum of action.

The idea that we must get *swaraj* [independence] is knowledge, and the person who possesses it is the knower; but this is not enough to bring us *swaraj*. There should be corresponding work for *swaraj* — the means of winning it. We can think out similar instances of any class of activities.

(19) Knowledge, action, and the doer are of three kinds according to their different *gunas*. Hear thou these, just as they have been described in the science of the *gunas*.

(20) Know that knowledge whereby one sees in all beings immutable entity — a unity in diversity — to be *sattvic*.

Things in this world seem distinct from one another, but in reality they are not so. If the jaundice in our eyes disappears, we would see all things as one undivided reality.

(21) That knowledge which perceives separately in all beings several entities of diverse kinds, know thou to be *rajas*.

That knowledge is *rajasic* which perceives separately in all beings different entities of various kinds. It is through the *rajas* spirit that we make these three classes — I, mine and others. Attachments and aversions arise from this. The *sattvic* state has no room for attachments and aversions.

---

(22) And knowledge which, without reason, clings to one single thing as though it were everything, which misses the true essence and is superficial is *tamas*.

Tamas jnana is that in virtue of which a person does everything with attachment, without seeing any purpose in what he does, and believing that it is without significance and of no consequence. In *tamas* knowledge, all kinds of notions are mixed up and it is believed that there is no such Being as God.

(23) That action is called *sattvic* which, being one's allotted task, is performed without attachment, without like or dislike, and without a desire for fruit.

(24) That action which is prompted by the desire for fruit or by the thought of "I", and which involves much dissipation of energy is called *rajas*.

A *sattvic* person does not go seeking work. A *rajasic* person is engaged one day in inventing an aeroplane and is busy the next in discovering how to reach India from England in five hours. Such a person sets apart half an hour out of twenty-four to deceive his *Atman*, and devotes the remaining twenty-three and a half to his body.

Is the *charkha* work [spinning] *rajasic*, or is it *sattvic*, too? This can be decided only by reference to the spirit in which it is done. If a person plies the *charkha* merely for the sake of money, his work is *rajasic*; but it will be *sattvic* if he does so for the good of the world, in the spirit of a *yajna*.

(25) That action which is blindly undertaken without any regard to capacity and consequences, involving loss and hurt, is called *tamas*.

In *tamas*, a person plunges into work without thinking of the consequences. One who works without desiring the fruit of his work knows what that fruit will be, but does not yearn for it.

(26) That doer is called *sattvic* who has shed all attachment, all sense of "I", who is filled with firmness and zeal, and who recks neither success nor failure.

Free from the sense of "I" means one who works merely as an instrument. To say that he should have no attachment does not mean that he should be indifferent. On the contrary, such a person should be more active than others.

Do the British officials who come out to India lack anything in endurance and energy? They seem to be *yogis*, but they are not free from attachment. They believe in ends, and will adopt any means, fair or foul, for their sake; but one who is free from attachment is concerned with nothing but work and displays unfailing determination and energy. A person who works in this spirit is a *sattvic* doer.

(27) That doer is said to be *rajas* who is passionate, desirous of the fruit of action, greedy, violent, unclean, and easily excited by joy or sorrow in success or failure.

(28) The doer is called *tamas* who is undisciplined, vulgar, stubborn, knavish, lacking firmness of decision, indolent, woebegone and dilatory.

(29) Hear now, O Dhananjaya, detailed fully and severally, the threefold division of understanding and will, according to their *gunas*.

(30) That understanding, O Partha, is *sattvic* which knows
action from inaction, what ought to be done from what
ought not to be done, bondage from release, which things
one should guard against and of which things one need
have no fear.

(31) That understanding, O Partha, is *rajas* which decides
erroneously between right and wrong, between what ought
to be done and what ought not to be done.

(32) That understanding, O Partha, is *tamas* which,
shrouded in darkness, thinks wrong to be right and sees
everything in a wrong light.

(33) That will, O Partha, is *sattvic* which, by *yoga*, main-
tains an unbroken harmony between the activities of the
mind, the vital energies and the senses.

If a person clings to the decision he has made without
being exercised about the consequences, does not change it from
day to day, then we may say that he possesses a will that is
unbroken. "By *yoga*" means in a spirit of dedication to God.

(34) That will, O Partha, is *rajas* which clings with attachment to righteousness, desire and wealth, desirous of fruit
in each case.

"Righteousness" signifies dedication to God and "desire"
attachment. Because of that attachment, one pursues *dharma*,

wealth, power and pleasure. The decision of such a person may be faulty.

(35) That will, O Partha, is *tamas* whereby insensate man does not abandon sleep, fear, grief, despair and self-conceit.

Everything we do involves grief and ignorance, and, at any rate, disappointment and fear.

(36) Hear now from Me, O Bharatarshabha, the three kinds of pleasure. Pleasure which is enjoyed only by repeated practice, and which puts an end to pain;

(37) Which, in its inception, is as poison, but in the end as nectar born of the serene realization of the true nature of *Atman* — that pleasure is said to be *sattvic*.

One must do *tapascharya* [austerities] for such happiness. It involves renunciation and, therefore, means hardship in the beginning. Everything in which one must sacrifice sleep and give up lethargy, for instance study and learning and teaching, is a kind of *tapascharya*; but the reward is knowledge of the Self. The bliss of knowing the *Atman* is of the same character as the *Atman*. The happiness of the body comes wholly from the satisfaction of desires, and because it depends on the satisfaction of desires it is transient. It is as transient as the life of a butterfly or a flash of lightning. The other happiness abides forever.

(38) That pleasure is called *rajas* which, arising from the contact of the senses with their objects, is at first as nectar but in the end like poison.

Suppose we have been to a play or some such show. We enjoy witnessing it, but afterwards suffer for loss of sleep and also on account of the effect of the play on our mind.

(39) That pleasure is called *tamas* which, arising from sleep and sloth and heedlessness, stupefies the soul both at first and in the end.

(40) There is no being, either on earth or in heaven among the gods, that can be free from these three *gunas* born of *prakriti*.

We should, therefore, strive to become free from these.

(41) The duties of Brahmins, Kshatriyas, Vaisyas and Sudras are distributed according to their innate qualifications, O Parantapa.

(42) Serenity, self-restraint, austerity, purity, forgiveness, uprightness, knowledge and discriminative knowledge, and faith in God are the Brahmin's natural duties.

Serenity, self-restraint, *tapas* (to keep body, speech and mind under control by hard discipline), purity, forgiveness (to wish well, from the heart, even to a person who may have hit us with a stone), straightforwardness (to have no impurity in one's eyes, to behave decently), knowledge and knowledge based on experience (not bookish, dry knowledge), faith in God — these are the natural duties of the Brahmin.

A person may have the qualities enumerated above, but may not believe in God, may be lacking in faith and devotion; if so, those very qualities will prove harmful. For instance, in Europe these days they train the body for prize competitions and wrestling matches. These persons, too, are required to exercise discipline over the body, but that is done without devotion to God and helps them in no way. Hence belief in and devotion to God should be among the most important characteristics of a Brahmin.

(43) Valor, spiritedness, constancy, resourcefulness, not fleeing from battle, being always ready to help the poor, and the capacity to rule are the natural duties of a Kshatriya.

A Brahmin, too, should have these qualities. Likewise, a Kshatriya should have the qualities of a Brahmin. In this way every individual should display, in varying measure, the qualities associated with all the castes, and a person will belong to the case whose virtues he possesses in a predominant measure. These will determine his natural *karmas*.

(44) Tilling the soil, protection of the cow and commerce are the natural functions of a Vaisya, while service is the natural duty of a Sudra.

(45) Each man, by complete absorption in the performance of his duty, wins perfection. Hear now how he wins such perfection by devotion to that duty.

(46) By offering the worship of his duty to Him who is the moving spirit of all beings, and by Whom all this is pervaded, man wins perfection.

Anyone who worships the *Atman* — the *Brahman*, God that exists pervading the universe like its warp and woof — reaches the goal. True success crowns him alone who sees prayer or worship in the *karma* which has fallen to his lot as his duty, who has made service and every *karma* of his a form of prayer.

(47) Better *karma* which is one's duty, though uninviting, than *karma* which is somebody else's duty which may be more easily performed. Doing duty which accords with one's nature, one incurs no sin.

The central teaching of the Gita is detachment — abandonment of the fruit of action. And there would be no room for this abandonment if one were to prefer another's duty to one's own. Therefore one's own duty is said to be better than another's. It is the spirit in which duty is done that matters, and its unattached performance is its own reward.

(48) One should not abandon, O Kaunteya, that duty which has come to one unsought, imperfect though it be; for all action, in its inception, is enveloped in imperfection, as fire in smoke.

This does not apply to actions like stealing. It applies only to actions which have been described in the preceding verses as the natural *karmas* of the four castes. Even if one sees some evil in such *karmas* — as, for instance, Arjuna's shrinking from fighting because of his weakness of attachment — it is best to do them, for every *karma*, every beginning, is tainted with some evil.

(49) He who has given up attachment to everything, who is master of himself, who is dead to desire, attains through *sannyasa* the supreme perfection of freedom from action.

Here by *sannyasa* is meant not renunciation of all *karmas* but only the renunciation of the fruit of all *karmas,* and it is such renunciation alone which can be successfully practiced.

(50) Learn now from Me, in brief, O Kaunteya, how he who has gained this perfection attains to *Brahman,* the supreme consummation of knowledge.

(51) Equipped with purified understanding, restraining the self with firm will, abandoning sound and other objects of the senses, putting aside likes and dislikes,

(52) Living in solitude, spare in diet, restrained in speech, body and mind, ever absorbed in *dhyana yoga* [meditation], anchored in dispassion,

(53) Without pride, violence, arrogance, lust, wrath, possession, having shed all sense of "mine" and at peace with himself, he is fit to become one with *Brahman.*

Ahankar, bala and *darpa* [pride, violence and arrogance] include one another, but it would not be like the Gita to use only one term. Its manner is to say the same thing over and over again in different ways.

About *laghvashi* [spare in diet]: I observe the vow of taking not more than five articles in my daily food, but even if I keep it literally, I have not succeeded in keeping it well. Haridas gave me some dates as a gift. He watched my mood and offered me one to eat. I relished it, and immediately became conscious of a lapse. I told myself, "You eat more than others do." I ate the date and it stuck in my throat. This is what should happen if we treat the body as something out of which we must take work.

In these verses, we are asked to purify the intellect and to be *laghvashi*. To be *laghvashi* does not mean merely to be moderate in eating, but to be satisfied with one article when we feel we can make do with two. It is as though this misfortune befell me because we would be discussing the word *laghvashi* today.

(54) One with *Brahman* and at peace with himself, he grieves not, nor desires. Holding all beings alike, he achieves supreme devotion to Me.

(55) By devotion he realizes in truth how great I am, Who I am, and having known Me in reality he enters into Me.

(56) Even while always performing actions, he who makes Me his refuge wins, by My grace — not through his own strength — the eternal and imperishable haven.

(57) Casting with thy mind all actions on Me, make Me thy goal, and resorting to the *yoga* of even-mindedness, knowledge and meditation, fix thy thought ever on Me.

(58) Fixing thus thy thought on Me, thou shalt surmount all obstacles by My grace; but if possessed by the sense of "I" thou listen not, thou shalt perish.

(59) If obsessed by the sense of "I", thou thinkest, "I will not fight," vain is thy obsession. Thy nature will compel thee.

(60) What thou will not do, O Kaunteya, because of thy delusion, thou shalt do, even against thy will, bound as thou art by the duty to which thou art born.

"Hence," says Shri Krishna, "dedicate everything to Me and, free from attachments and aversions and ever devoted to me, do the task which has fallen to your lot. So acting you will remain untouched by sin."

(61) God, O Arjuna, dwells in the heart of every being and to His delusive mystery whirls them all, as the clay on the potter's wheel.

We are sitting on this ball of earth, which does not stop from rotating or revolving even for a moment. It keeps rotating and revolving all the twenty-four hours. The stars and the sun do the same. Thus, nothing in the world is motionless. But things do not move through their own power. It is God's power which keeps everything in motion.

Just as we keep a machine in motion only as long as we choose and it has no power of its own to move, so also does God keep us in motion as He wills. We should not, therefore, be proud that we have done something. We should shed our egotism, become as a machine in God's hand and carry out His will — look upon Him as our all and obey His plan.

(62) In Him alone seek thy refuge with all thy heart, O Bharata. By His grace shalt thou win to the eternal haven of supreme peace.

(63) Thus have I expounded to thee the most mysterious of all knowledge. Ponder over it fully, then act as thou wilt.

(64) Hear again My supreme word, the most mysterious of all. Dearly beloved thou art of Me, hence I desire to declare thy welfare.

(65) On Me fix thy mind. To Me bring thy devotion. To Me offer thy sacrifice. To Me make thy obeisance. To Me indeed shalt thou come. Solemn is My promise to thee: thou art dear to Me.

(66) Abandon all duties and come to Me, the only refuge. I will release thee from all sins, grieve not!

This verse is the essence of all *shastras* and of the Gita. Shri Krishna tells Arjuna, "You should give up all arguing and take refuge in Me. That will be wholly for your supreme good. Only the service of the *Atman* will advance a person's welfare."

(67) Utter this knowledge never to him who knows no austerity, has no devotion, nor any desire to listen, nor yet to him who scoffs at Me.

(68) He who will propound this supreme mystery to My devotees, shall, by that act of highest devotion to Me, surely come to Me.

It is only he who has himself gained the knowledge and lived it in his life that can declare it to others. These two *shlokas* cannot possibly have any reference to him who can give a flaw-less reading and interpretation of the Gita while conducting himself anyhow.

(69) Nor among men is there any who renders dearer service to Me than he; nor shall there be on earth any more beloved by Me than he.

(70) And who so shall study this sacred discourse of ours shall worship Me with the sacrifice of knowledge. That is My belief.

That is, he who studies this intelligently will become free. Merely reciting the verses mechanically and without understanding their meaning will certainly not bring freedom.

(71) And the man of faith who, scorning not, will but listen to it — even he shall be released and will go to the happy worlds of men of virtuous deeds.

(72) Hast thou heard this, O Partha, with a concentrated mind? Has thy delusion, born of ignorance, been destroyed, O Dhananjaya?

Arjuna said:

(73) Thanks to Thy grace, O Achyuta, my delusion is destroyed. My understanding has returned. I stand secure, my doubts all dispelled. I will do Thy bidding.

Arjuna's memory, which had become clouded, has become clear. He has understood what his nature and his duty are, and his doubt has gone.

Sanjaya said:

(74) Thus did I hear this marvelous and thrilling discourse between Vasudeva and the great-souled Partha.

(75) It was by Vyasa's favor that I listened to this supreme and mysterious *yoga* as expounded by the lips of the Master of *Yoga*, Krishna Himself.

(76) O King, as often as I recall that marvelous and purifying discourse between Keshava and Arjuna, I am filled with recurring rapture.

If we do not feel a new interest in this every time we read it, the fault must lie with us, it cannot be that of the author of the Gita.

(77) And as often as I recall that marvelous form of Hari, my wonder knows no bounds and I rejoice again and again.

(78) Wheresoever Krishna, the Master of *Yoga*, is, and wheresoever is Partha the Bowman, there, rest assured, are Fortune, Victory, Prosperity and Eternal Right.

To Shri Krishna has been attached the epithet Yogeshvar [Master of *Yoga*] and to Arjuna Dhanurdhara [Bowman]. This means that there are fortune, victory and eternal right only where there is perfect knowledge joined with light and power. He who has knowledge should have the fullest strength to use it. There should be perfection of knowledge and it should be fully translated into action. For that person who has the strength of spirit to act upon what seems certain knowledge to him, there is no such thing as defeat. If he goes on acting in that spirit, even his errors will be corrected in course of time.

We know that we should always speak the truth, but manage to tell only half the truth; but he who has pure knowledge and the necessary energy to act upon it, that is, has taken up bow and arrow, will never depart from the path of morality.

We do not intend to give up the reading of the Gita. Its reading at prayer time will continue, a few verses everyday. We may also discuss some of them again, if we wish to. This is a work which persons belonging to all faiths can read. It does not favor any sectarian point of view. It teaches nothing but pure ethics.

The conclusion of our study of the Gita is that we should pray and read holy books, and know our duty and do it. If any book can help, it is this. Really, however, what help can a book or a commentary on it give? In the end, we achieve only as much as it is our good fortune to do. Our only right is to *purushartha* [determined effort]. We can only strive and work All human beings, and animals too, struggle. The only difference is that we believe that behind our struggle there is an intelligent purpose What is the purpose, however? Merely to keep alive this body, or to know that which has taken on this body? To raise it or advance it, if that is possible?

For the first object we work in any case, whether we wish or no. Our body itself is so made that it makes us work for it, even if we are unwilling. For instance, while the baby is still in the mother's womb, its organs do function in one way or another. Though unconsciously, it does breathe. That also is a kind of effort, but it is not *purushartha*. Only effort aimed at the welfare of the *Atman* can be described as *purushartha*.

It has been described as the supreme *purushartha*. All else is futile expenditure of energy. For such *purushartha*, one of the means is reading the *shastras* and reflecting and meditating on them. In order that our study may be really useful, it is necessary to repeat our recitation over and over again with attention to pronunciation, rhythm, etc. It is necessary to create an atmosphere of holiness round the Gita.

The truth about ourselves is that we strive for supreme *purushartha* and know how to seek the means for it. We should honor and revere the Gita. It will certainly protect us. It is a deity of the mind. If so, we should read it daily as a part of our prayer.

Bibliography

Many editions of the Bhagavad Gita and many useful books about Gandhi are available in English. The following works were most frequently consulted for guidance in the preparation of *The Bhagavad Gita Gita According to Gandhi*.

Aurobindo, Sri. *The Bhagavad Gita,* With Text, Translation and Commentary. Edited by Parmeshwari Prasad Khetan. Sri Aurobindo Divine Life Trust, 1995.

Bhave, Vinoba, *Talks on the Gita,* Sarva Seva Sangh Prakashan, 1970.

Desai, Mahadev. *The Gospel of Selfless Action, or The Gita According to Gandhi.* Translation of the original in Gujarati, with an additional introduction and commentary. Navajivan Publishing House, 1946.

Easwaran, Eknath. *The Bhagavad Gita.* With chapter introductions by Diana Morrison, Nilgiri Press, 1996.

— *Gandhi The Man: The Story of His Transformation.* Nilgiri Press, 2000.

Feuerstein, Georg. *The Shambhala Guide to Yoga.* Shambhala, 1996.

Fischer, Louis. *The Life of Mahatma Gandhi.* Harper & Row, 1950.

Gandhi, Mahatma. *An Autobiography: The Story of My Experiments with Truth.* Beacon Press, 1993.

— *The Collected Works of Mahatma Gandhi,* volume XXXII (1926-

1927), "Discourses on the Gita", pp. 94-377. The Publications Division, Ministry of Information and Broadcasting, Government of India. 1969.

Mascaro, Juan. *The Bhagavad Gita.* Translated from the Sanskrit with an Introduction. Penguin, 1973.

Morrison, Diana. *A Glossary of Sanskrit from the Spiritual Tradition of India.* Nilgiri Press, 1977.

Nanda, B. R. *Mahatma Gandhi: A Biography.* Barron's, 1965.

Prabhavananda, Swami and Christopher Isherwood. *How to Know God: The Yoga Aphorisms of Patanjali.* Vedanta Press, 1996.

Radhakrishnan, Sarvepalli. *The Bhagavad Gita.* With an Introductory Essay, Sanskrit Text, English Translation, and Notes. HarperCollins Publishers India, 1993.

Tendulkar, Dinanath Gopal. *Mahatma: The Life of Mohandas Karamchand Gandhi* (Eight volumes). Publications Division, Ministry of Information and Broadcasting, Government of India, 1960-66.

Vanamali. *The Play of God: Visions of the Life of Krishna.* Blue Dove Press, 1996.

Glossary and Index

yajna — Sacrifice; offering. 60, 63-67, 85, 92-96, 99, 102, 135-137, 153, 221

yama-niyama — Cardinal and casual vows. The five cardinal vows are: nonviolence, truth, non-stealing, celibacy and non-possession. The five casual vows: are bodily purity, contentment, the study of the scriptures, austerity and meditation of God. 112, 202

yoga — Union; spiritual practice or discipline; sometimes, action. 44-50, 59-62, 71, 78, 93-94, 99-106, 111-115, 118-129, 138, 139, 145, 154-155, 158, 179-180, 187, 199, 205, 223, 228-229, 233

yogi — One who undertakes spiritual disciplines

Epithets of Krishna and Arjuna

Krishna

Achyuta — Unfailing

Arisudana — Slayer of foes

Govinda — Herdsman

Hari — He who takes hold of

Hrishikesha — Lord of the senses

Jagannivasa — Refuge of the Universe

Janardana — Liberator of Men

Kamala-Patraksha — Lotus-eyed

Keshava — Having fine hair

Keshinsudana — Slayer of Keshin

Madhava — The husband of the goddess Lakshmi

Madhusudana — Slayer of the demon Madhu

Purushottama — All-pervading

Varshneya — Descendant of Vrishni

Vasudeva — Son of Vasudeva; All-pervading

Vishnu — All-pervading

Yadava — Descendant of Yadu

Arjuna

Bharata — Descendent of Bharata

Bharatarshabha — Best of Bharatas

Bharatasattama — Best of Bharatas

Bharatashreshtha — Best of Bharatas

Gudakesha — One who wears their hair in a ball
Dhananjaya — Winner of wealth
Kaunteya — Son of Kunti
Kurunandana — Scion of Kurus
Kurupravira — Hero of the Kurus
Kurusattama — Best of Kurus
Kurushreshtha — Best of Kurus
Pandava — Son of Pandu
Parantapa — Tormentor of foes
Partha — Son of Partha or Kunti

Contributors

M. K. GANDHI is regarded by many as a Hindu saint and the father of Indian independence. Born at Porbandar on October 2, 1869, he left India as a young man to study law in London. His legal career took him to South Africa in 1893, where he first became involved in political struggles, working to secure rights for Indian expatriates. He remained in South Africa for more than two decades, and it was during these years that his remarkable form of political reform through nonviolence, which he called Satyagraha, was born.

Upon his return to India, Gandhi assumed a leadership role in the fight for Indian independence from Great Britain. He also worked tirelessly for religious toleration in India, which was divided by Hindu-Moslem antagonism, and for the destruction of the caste system, which codified class conflicts in ancient religious terms. Gandhi's role emerged not only as that of a political revolutionary, but also as a religious leader. As he insisted, he was a man of God first.

Indian independence from Britain was finally achieved on August 15, 1947. Five months later, on January 25, 1948, Gandhi was assassinated by a conservative Hindu.

MICHAEL N. NAGLER is Professor Emeritus of Classics and Comparative Literature at the University of California, Berkeley. He is the founder and chairperson of the University's Peace and Conflict Studies Program, and currently teaches courses in nonviolence and meditation. Dr. Nagler is the author of *America Without Violence*, and, with Eknath Easwaran, an English edition of *The Upanishads,* as well as numerous articles on classics, myth, peace and mysticism. His book *Is There No Other Way?: The Search for a Nonviolent Future,* will be published by Berkeley Hills Books in Fall 2000. He lives in Tomales, California.

JOHN STROHMEIER is the editor of four works by Mahatma Gandhi, including *Prayer, Vows and Observances,* and *Book of Prayers,* and co-author of *Divine Harmony: The Life and Teachings of Pythagoras.* He lives in Berkeley, California. He may be reached by email at: jpstroh@berkeleyhills.com.

For other titles in the Berkeley Hills Books series of works by Mahatma Gandhi, please contact your bookseller, call us toll-free at (888) 848-7303, or see www.berkeleyhills.com.

Prayer
A collection of Gandhi's most important writings on the methods and power of prayer, including Ramanama, the repetition of the name of God. ISBN: 1-893163-09-1

Book of Prayers
Selections from Gandhi's *Ashram Bhajanavali*, the prayer book of Satyagraha Ashram. Translated into English by Gandhi for his western followers. ISBN: 1-893163-02-4

Vows and Observances
Gandhi's writings on the "Eleven Observances," the rules for daily living of Satyagraha Ashram. ISBN: 1-893163-01-6

The Way to God
Selections from Gandhi's writings on the nature of God and spiritual practice. ISBN: 1-893163-00-8